M000087927

HOW YOU CAN MAKE A FORTUNE SELLING INFORMATION BY MAIL

By

Russ von Hoelscher

Profit Ideas
Escondido, CA

This book is dedicated to my friends and clients, Eileen and T.J. Rohleder. They have proven that you really can make a fortune selling information by mail, starting from scratch.

One good idea (combining the power of mail order information selling with passive telemarketing. A simple telephone answering machine)˙ took them from almost zero to millions of dollars in book and manual sales in less than two years. It could not have happened to a nicer couple.

—Russ von Hoelscher

"By the way, what are you doing to become a hero? Don't blush at your greatness, actualize it!"

—Alfred Korzybski

TABLE OF CONTENTS

Chapter 4: Specialize your Mail Order Venture—Offer "Related Information" 63

Chapter 5: How to Get the Best Job at the Best Price From Printers 73

Chapter 6: How to Reduce Mailing Expenses, Plus How to Determine Your Customer's Worth. 89

PREFACE

This is the Age Of Information. Today, the Information Industry is expanding at an incredible pace. It is out-performing the GNP by over 100%. Many entrepreneurs have already made their fortune in the 1980s with new information ventures, and many more will strike it rich during the 1990s and beyond.

Just as there are many ways to package information (books, manuals, reports, newsletters, audio or visual tapes, computer programs, etc.), there are also several ways to sell information (in retail stores, at select information retrieval centers, etc.). However, one method offers the greatest potential for national or international sales, and that's mail order selling.

Mail order, or Direct Marketing, as it is now often called, is experiencing unprecedented growth. Much of this growth is directly related to the marketing techniques used by more and more information entrepreneurs.

This book will acquaint you with many of the rich, new opportunities available in information marketing.

You will learn how to make money advertising and selling simple, yet vital information by mail to eager buyers all over the United States and Canada, and in some cases, to buyers worldwide.

For over 20 years I have been researching, discovering, developing, and/or creating the best moneymaking methods ordinary men and women can use to make extraordinary sums of money. Now that the information age has taken center stage, I want to present you with many ways in which you can prosper by selling information by mail. And you don't have to be intimidated by the modern metal monster known as the computer. You can make money, and lots of it, selling information, as I have for many years, without being a computer whiz. Truth is, I'm just beginning to understand a few things about these amazing, yet complex, mechanical brains.

If you're completely computer illiterate, it may not be a bad idea to enroll in a low tuition night school class to obtain some hands-on experience. However, it is not essential to your success. I know information age marketing entrepreneurs who have made millions without ever knowing how to turn on a computer, much less operate one. Fact is, I know some very well-to-do information by mail sellers who don't even know how to use a typewriter.

This book isn't concerned with making money with information and retrieval systems. It's about making money by developing, packaging and then selling information by mail. Vital information and powerful mail order marketing strategies are a perfect match. Knowing how to obtain the one (the information) and use the other (mail order) to sell can make you a fortune. And that's what this book is all about.

You deserve Total Success,

Russ von Hoelscher

Section I
THE BASICS

Chapter 1

HOW TO FIND SALEABLE "INFORMATION PRODUCTS"

Once you decide information marketing is for you, and you are ready to start (do not get started until you have read this book twice and have ordered and studied at least some of the other support material—books, guides, reports, etc.—I recommend later in this book), then it's time to create or locate your information products (books, directories, reports, cassette tapes, etc.). Since we'll spend a good deal of space defining the creation of information products, let's start by talking about finding saleable items that are already in existence.

FINDING ITEMS TO SELL

There are hundreds of publishers who will be most eager to have you sell their books, reports, and other paper-and-ink products. (See wholesale and dropship book and information dealers listed in the "Source Directory" section of this book.) Several mail order information sellers cut their teeth by selling other publishers' wares by mail, often via the dropship method.

THE PROS AND CONS OF DROPSHIPPING

Dropshipping is an often used (by companies both large and small) marketing method that allows a dealer to sell a product, collect the money, usually in advance, then have the product shipped to the buyer by another source (usually the manufacturer, importer, major distributor or publisher). In book and information marketing circles, the dropship dealer receives full payment in advance, keeps his or her percentage, most often 50% of the money, and then sends the other 50% of the money plus a shipping label made out to the customer, to the prime source. The prime source, who is often, but not necessarily, the publisher of the item sold, puts the item (the book, report or whatever) into a shipping bag or box, puts on the dropship dealer's label, adds postage, and mails it to the dealer's customer.

On the pro side, it's a very easy, and relatively low-cost way to get involved with mail selling. The dealer doing business via the dropship method carries no inventory. His only concern is getting the order. Once orders come in, he keeps his percentage and sends them onto the prime source for fulfillment. Of course, it's important that you deal with a reliable source that can and does ship orders promptly.

The "con side" of dropshipping is this: although it can be a great source of additional profits for many mail order book and information sellers, who, via the dropship method, can offer a wider range of items to their customers, very few dealers can run a business profitably solely by dropship selling. The reason is, the 50% (one half of money received) is usually not enough to keep a business in black ink. A profit margin of 200% or larger is often considered necessary in the information by mail business. And some operators constantly strive for gross markups of 500% and more.

I love the dropship method, and it works well for many information dealers. However, it's not my recommendation that you use it as your only source of income.

16

Your main profit center must be built around information products you create and control and/or purchase, at deep discounts, for resale.

HOW TO BUY AT DEEP DISCOUNTS

Once you have selected the type of books, reports, directories, or other information products you want to sell, write on your letterhead to all publishers who carry the kind of material you wish to promote. Perhaps the publisher's literature for dealers only mentions dropshipping or small discounts for quantity purchases. Don't be too concerned with prices quoted to you. If you see items that turn you on, request samples (sometimes they will be free; often you'll have to pay 50% off regular prices).

If after reviewing an item, you're certain you want to sell it, pick up your phone and call the supply source. Almost everything in life is negotiable. Printed price sheets are definitely *not* the last word in how much you should pay. They are only a point to begin discussion.

Obviously, you must give something to get something. Although I have often obtained a much better price on even a small order, you're more likely to obtain a deep discount on large orders.

The secret to getting a good price lies in being a good negotiator. The key factors in being a good negotiator are always found in your ability to remain calm, friendly and persistent throughout your buy/sell discussions. People usually want to make a deal, and usually will consider any offer that lets them make a deal, and at least some profit.

What constitutes a deep discount? Recently I purchased a book by mail order from another publisher. The book sold for $14.95 retail and his dealer's price sheet called for a wholesale price of $6.00 per copy (only a 60% discount on orders of 100 copies). Not enough markup for my liking. After 10 minutes of serious, but friendly negotiating, it was agreed I could buy 200 copies at $3.75 per copy. That gave me a nice 300% markup. We both had no regrets on the deal, even though his price sheet stated $3.75 was his lowest wholesale price, and then only for orders of 1,000 copies or more. I made a good deal, but then I usually do. So can you!

I regard prices on a wholesale price sheet, the same way I regard prices on both new and used automobiles. Although some car dealers won't budge an inch, the majority will take a lot less than the sticker asks for.

In my dealings with publishers, manufacturers and distributors over the years, I find no more than 20% of them hold firm, while at least 80% are willing to give a little—or a lot!

BIG VALUES AND PROFITS IN REMAINDERS

If you can get good deals buying from other publishers, and you often can, you'll be very pleased at the big values available in remainder books. In some cases you'll be able to purchase books and manuals for as little as 10% or 15% of cover prices. This gives you a great markup. In the "Source Directory" section of this book I present you with several leading remainder dealers. The key to success here is to find nonfiction and reasonably current information titles which are available in good supply, and at a great price.

I have found that titles that enjoyed impressive bookstore sales, before being overprinted, can often be turned into mail order winners.

Ralph Ginzburg, publisher of *American Business* and *Moneysworth*, is a master at the art of snatching up good remainder titles and turning them into mail order winners. Several other sharp operators are also active in this field.

An often asked question is: "Why would a book or manual that once sold well in bookstores but now is no longer in big demand be a potential fast mail order seller? The answer will surprise many. This author has been very active in mail order and direct marketing for over twenty years. I also have owned nine different bookstores. Fact: only a relatively small number of mail order nonfiction book and information buyers are regular bookstore customers. I have discovered most bookshop clients are insatiable readers and book lovers, where the majority of mail order information responders do not possess strong feelings about books per se, but rather purchase books, manuals, directories, reports, tapes, etc., only when so motivated by a strong direct mail piece or a powerful ad, and only because of the information value to the mail order buyer.

You can hand-pick the "diamonds" from the acres of dandelions (less than 2% of remainder books available are potential big mail order winners). Just remember to consider only those materials that contain "how to" instructions or information likely to be in demand by today's information-hungry mail order buyer. In almost every case, all forms of fiction, poetry, biographies, coffee table books, etc., should not be considered.

A few years ago I was given the opportunity to purchase thousands of copies of remainder hardcover books—all fiction by leading authors (Harold Robbins, Rosemary Rogers, Jackie Collins, etc.)—at only 5¢ on the retail dollar. $14.95 books would cost me just 75¢ each; $19.95 books only $1.00 each. Truly, a great price. Nevertheless, I turned the deal down. It's not really a good deal unless you know how to sell it. I know how to sell information by mail. I'll leave fiction, poetry and the like for somebody else. I suggest you do likewise.

BIDDING FOR CLOSEOUTS

The best possible price available for remainder books goes to the dealer who bids and buys the entire stock from a publisher. This is essentially what remainder distributors do. Example: After a year or more of brisk sales, book sales drop drastically on a certain book. The publisher takes inventory and finds they have, let's say, 3,304 copies on hand. Often this publisher will send a notice to several remainder distributors on their mailing list and request bids on this title. The bid to cover purchase of all copies left. In this case, 3,304 copies of a retail $20.00 book.

If you wanted this title for mail order, you could be among the bidders if you were on this publisher's closeout bidders list (several major publishers' addresses are listed in the *Source Directory*). How much would you pay?

A friend of mine who will remain unnamed, an executive with Simon & Schuster, informs me that the winning bid on a quantity of closeouts is usually between 3% and 7% of cover. This means it would be possible to purchase all 3,304 copies of our hypothetical $20.00 closeout book for as little as 60¢ each. Would you like to buy 3,304 copies of a $20.00 book that would sell fast by mail for as little as 60¢ each? It has been done and will continue to be done. Why not you?

Several years ago, Healthmark Publications in Minneapolis purchased 2,500 copies of a health manual at a deep discount, via the closeout· method. All copies quickly sold by mail. Since demand was so very high, they hated to see that last book shipped. What to do now? They needed more books to sell! It was decided if they couldn't buy more copies, they would be willing to reprint the book. A deal was struck with the original publisher, who was willing to accept a modest royalty. Over the next two years, 40,000 books were printed and sold.

Yes! It's possible to make money—and lots of it—with items that, at first glance, appear to no longer have great selling appeal.

The retail book trade and the mail order marketplace are two vastly different sales arenas. Although I've made good money over the years selling books to bookstores, libraries, and to other traditional book outlets, it has been peanuts compared to the big money available in mail order.

Purchasing books and other printed matter from others is a legitimate, and potentially profitable way to enter the lucrative world of book and information marketing by mail.

Personally, I like to do both: create (write and publish) and locate additional materials someone else has produced.

Chapter 2

CREATING (SELF-PUBLISHING) SALEABLE " PAPER AND INK" PRODUCTS

Although books are just one form of saleable information, I will often use the words "books" in my writings. When you see the word book, or books, mentioned, you may wish to substitute the term, "paper and ink products." The information seeker isn't too concerned about how the vehicle (the paper and ink) is packaged (a directory, report, book, newsletter, etc.). What *is* important is the information. Will it make her or him richer or enhance one's health? Will it ease the person's workload or provide leisure time for fun? Will it provide required data or help the individual obtain more dates? People are searching for thousands of different ways to obtain more benefits and make their lives more happy, productive and meaningful. Discover a need and fill it, or create a need and satisfy it. Either way, they'll send their money.

You don't have to be a "gifted" writer to make big money with information.

This manual is written for anyone who would like to earn money, a little extra dough or whole bunches of long green, through a process of *SELLING INFORMATION.*

Ernest Hemingway, John Steinbeck, James Jones, Taylor Caldwell and William Shakespeare are *writers.* I'm just a pencil-pushing word seller, but I'm making nice money and enjoying myself. And you can, too.

I have prospered by writing and/or "packaging" well over three dozen books and manuals, but only one of them, to date, *How to Achieve Total Success,* qualifies as a work of art. Through a constant process of daily meditation and the practice of advanced *Mind Science* principles, I believe I was inspired during the six month period in which I wrote that book. I'm very proud of *Total Success*, and the positive effect it has had and continues to have, on lives all over the world. I'm also pleased with the success and profits generated from dozens of other practical business and investment works, that I have produced in something less than an "inspired" state of mind and being.

My advice: Get started on your information project. Don't wait for inspiration. There is more preparation involved in writing, researching or obtaining printed products, than inspiration. Add to that the importance of acquiring a sense of what can be promoted and sold by mail.

Don't let the "experts" trick you into thinking that you need an impressive training period and many years of formal education to write for pay. That's pure *horse manure!*

A positive mental attitude and an unyielding desire to succeed and "see it in print"—plus a willingness to share useful information can make you a winner in word-selling, information by mail business.

I offer no miracles, but in this manual you will find the techniques, tactics, concepts, guidelines and methods that can point you to success in writing and/or self-publishing. And that's all you need to enter and prosper in this fascinating arena.

ALWAYS GIVE THANKS FOR ALL THAT YOU ARE,

ALL THAT YOU ARE NOT AND ALL THAT YOU ARE
BECOMING.

FINDING SUBJECTS TO WRITE ABOUT AND PUBLISH

A work of fiction or a spiritual or Mind Science presentation must be brought forth from deep within the author's being. To be successful, it must reek with originality. Good, solid nonfiction works must also be spiced with creativity; however, here the author relies heavily upon research and/or past experiences to produce a strong manuscript. With many forms of information selling, you simply present the facts in plain English.

Information subject matter for directories, reports, booklets or full size books can be found anywhere and everywhere. For the very best results start with your own field of expertise or one you wish to read about and research. Don't kid me or yourself. If you're an adult who has not led a totally secluded life, you have useful information on a subject or subjects that folks will pay you to learn.

Here is a partial list of what people want to be, do and have.

PEOPLE'S WANTS AND DESIRES

People Want To Be:	People Want To Have:	People Want To Do:
Informed	Happiness	Live longer
Loved	More money	Their own thing
Appreciated	Advancement in business	Start their own business
Admired	Security for the future	Express their individuality
Beautiful	More leisure time	Accomplish something
Creative	Improved health	important
Powerful	Self-esteem	Obtain affection & love
Respected	Peace of mind	Important tasks
Productive	Self-control	Have fun
Desired	Pleasure	Travel to exciting places
Free	Improved physical	Enjoy life
Successful	appearance	Do less work
Recognized	More personal prestige	Make a meaningful
Forgiven	A positive image	contribution

Focus on providing people with simple, understandable,

and helpful information that will satisfy any of the above, or combination of the above. People will appreciate it, want it, and they will send their money.

As both a writer/publisher and mail order/direct marketing advertising consultant, I never cease to be amazed at the huge number of folks who have valuable information between their ears who don't consider packaging and selling it. Some just keep giving it away free, or much worse, they keep it to themselves. Dumb. This is the perfect time to get rich selling special information.

This is the age of specialized information. People are ready, willing and able to pay good money for zillions of different forms of useful knowledge. Simply find a need and fill it, or create the need and supply it.

Here's a meaningful exercise. Grab yourself paper and pen and write down every subject you have some degree of knowledge about. Don't bother putting these subject headings in any order of importance. Just jot them down as they drop down from your mind. After several minutes, when you begin groping for more headings, stop. Now examine your list and pick the topics that most interest you and get busy researching and writing!

THE TIME IS NOW!

"I just don't find time to write." The No. 1 cop-out of all would-be authors and information peddlers. Your success depends on effective use of your time!

You have heard the time-tested saying, "If you want something done, ask a busy person to do it." Busy, productive people who effectively manage their time will somehow get things done and meet their goals. At the same time the person who doesn't manage time will sit at the desk and stare at the work that should be done. Or perhaps shuffle papers without accomplishing anything, or quite likely, make excuses not to start at all.

Misuse of time seldom involves an isolated incident; it

almost always is part and parcel of a well-established pattern of poor work habits. God knows, changing or reprogramming our behavior is not an easy task. Learning to cope with the clock and make it work for us rather than against us is no simple behavior change. The potential pay-off is so beneficial, however, that we must turn destructive, time-wasting habits into rewarding habits that best utilize the precious gift that is time.

DOWN WITH CLUTTER

Many business people in general, and entrepreneurs in particular, have huge piles of papers, envelopes and current work on their desks, somehow assuming the more important matters, like cream, will rise to the top.

For some individuals some clutter actually seems to work. Since clutter has often been a part of my own experience, I have often rationalized it. "I'd go nuts if I had to maintain a tidy desk," is my plea to anyone who will listen. However, after getting serious about effective time management, I no longer can justify all my clutter and "piles." My desk is still never really neat and some clutter prevails; however, I have come a long way. I intend to continue to improve in this vital area and I strongly suggest you do likewise. I don't want to preach perfection, mind you, I just want all of us to avoid that chaotic, sinking feeling. Clutter can create tension and frustration; it can make us feel "hopelessly snowed under." That feeling can lead to unproductive work or escape. When a writer gets frustrated his work will be sub-par, if that person works at all. A work bottleneck is often followed by the mind shutting down. This is the "mental block" ploy that writers too often accept as an uncontrollable occurrence, thus giving it power in their experience. It is both avoidable and controllable. One excellent method to prevent the mental block syndrome is to keep both your desk and your mind free from excess clutter.

An effective means of dealing with your papers, projects, mail, etc., is to go through them and divide them into five categories:

(1) High Priority—Immediate Action
(2) Low Priority
(3) Pending
(4) Reading Matter
(5) Deep six it!

Put all high-priority items on top of your desk. Put all other items out of sight. Put them in your desk, under your desk or on a side table, in any case out of sight! (Naturally, all items in category five are already off your desk and in the circular file. Excellent time managers make liberal use of the wastebasket.) Your motto should be, *When in doubt, throw it out!*

Now sort through your high priority items and choose the one that ranks No. 1 in importance and have at it. Don't go on to anything else until this is accomplished, and so on and so on. When all top priority matters have been handled pull up the stack of low priority items and work on them.

YOUR WRITING TIMETABLE

One more crucial thought on your "high priority" list. Set aside a time to work exclusively on your current topic. It doesn't matter what particular writing or research task you are working on. What is important is that you set aside a certain period of time daily to accomplish it. If you can only spend two hours daily on our new "information business," at least spend those 2 hours wisely. Perhaps one hour will have to be spent on the business aspects of information selling. Set up a work schedule employing the five categories given. This would leave you with one hour daily (perhaps much more on weekends) to work on your chosen subject. For best results hold fast to this timetable and make it a daily routine. It is generally best to use the same work time each time (some writers do their best work very early in the mornings, others keep a pot of coffee brewing as they work into the wee hours of night). Find your best time and then stick with it. Most pros who write for a living (your ultimate goal?) keep a rigid schedule. My own "time to write" is both early and late. I have discovered 8 a.m. till 11 a.m. are three good morning hours for me, as are the late evening hours of 10 p.m. till around midnight. My concentration ebbs during "day-time hours" and I use my time for routine business activities.

PRIVACY IS A MUST

You need a time to research and write, plus you need a place to do it. If you already have an office in your home or a spare bedroom to turn into one, you have it made. If no such luxury exists, see if room exists in your garage—if it has adequate lighting, heat, etc. If all else fails, use your own bedroom evenings and put it off-limits to other family members for that hour or two in which you put words on paper. Some word sellers may set up shop on the kitchen table at night, but I have always felt the interruption factor there makes this household center a poor work area.

The kitchen table, for a start, is okay as a mail processing area if your writing is being marketed by mail—order—in which case, family members are not "off limits." Their help is strongly solicited and will be much appreciated. You may even consider letting "sonny" use the family car Saturday night if he licks enough stamps and stuffs enough envelopes, etc. How you bribe your spouse is your own concern. By now, you should know how to *push the right buttons.*

Single people make fine writers and information sellers. They also can conduct successful mail order businesses. The only thing they lack that a married person has (or should I say *may have*) is built-in cheap labor. The single person must either (1) do it himself or (2) hire outside help.

In all fairness there are advantages and disadvantages in both cases. Sure, your spouse and children love you. Still, a favor rendered means favors sought in return. Just think about all the trouble that boy might get into with your car Saturday night. On second thought, *don't* think about it!

STOP PROCRASTINATION— TAKE ACTION *NOW.*

The "I'll do it later" mentality prevents a multitude of great accomplishments. It robs you of time, money and true success. If procrastination is your problem, don't put off doing something about it!

The fundamental reason most people procrastinate is because they have formed a habit of avoiding responsibility. Again we must be willing to change old, unproductive habits. For the writer, here are three solid suggestions:

(1) Decide to change—starting NOW! Starting today (not tomorrow) set aside your time to write and handle related business matters.

(2) To find the necessary hours in a week for putting words on paper, willingly make the sacrifice. IN MANY CASES, SIMPLY CUTTING OUT OR CUTTING DOWN ON TV viewing (a major enemy of your Creative Force) will produce all the time you require to allow yourself to get set up in your new business.

(3) Don't give up. Too many people quit when they are drawing near a smashing success. Don't give up on yourself. You can do it! Also, if you find yourself slipping backward into old procrastinating habits, recognize your backsliding and take charge of your life. At first it may be two steps forward and one backward. If you continue to reinforce positive new success habits, you'll soon take ten strides forward for every tiny step back.

DON'T LET OTHERS WASTE YOUR TIME

Since most of us are masters at wasting our own time, we damn sure don't want outside help. You owe a certain amount of time to your family and friends. Strong marriages and true friendships require time and effort. Just remember, you must save some time for yourself and your business activities.

YOUR TIME IS NOW

Effective time management is of paramount importance to all success-minded people. For information business people, it is absolutely essential. I trust the time I have spent on this subject has not been in vain. By taking charge of the time in your life, you'll soon be *enjoying the time of your life!* **Guaranteed!**

WRITE YOUR AD FIRST

Although my advice on advertising will come later in this book, I wish to remind you here that you should write your ad before you write your book, report, directory, etc. This will keep you focused on your objective and will also serve as a reminder that your ads and/or direct mail package is first in importance in the information by mail business. While I always urge my students to offer a worthwhile paper and ink product that will completely satisfy the mail order responder, never forget your advertising message will make you or break you. To make big money selling information by mail, your ads have to stop readers dead in their tracks, totally capture their interest and motivate them to respond now! By mail, good advertising will sell a lot of poor to mediocre products, but poor ads cannot sell even the best products. Writing and publishing are much easier tasks than marketing. Or, as William Rickman of Kroch's and Brentano's so eloquently stated: *"It takes a certain brilliance to write a book, but it takes a genius to sell one."*

A STEP-BY-STEP GUIDE
TO PREPARING YOUR MANUSCRIPT

Preparation of a saleable "how to" information book, report or manual, or a directory of valuable information—addresses, etc.—need not be considered a monumental task. By dividing the components of a self-publishing project into a compiled order, you'll discover that a book or directory is put together one piece at a time.

A directory is usually the easiest project to undertake, once the information or addresses have been compiled. For example: if you decided to publish a directory of Hong Kong suppliers of merchandise of interest to American importers, you might invest considerable time and effort to research and obtain hundreds of names of Hong Kong manufacturers and distributors of various merchandise. However, once this information has been obtained, arranging your information into classifications and then having it typeset (or just neatly typed), and prepared for printing in a directory format, would be quite easy and require little imagination.

Preparing a *how-to* book is another matter. Let's suppose you are into metaphysical/psychological subjects, and would like to write a book titled, "How to Understand What Your Dreams Are Showing You" (*say, not a bad title for a book on the subject of dream analysis*). Now we are faced with a more complex project than a short report or a simply compiled directory. If you decide your dream book will be a *full-sized* one (generally considered to be 120 pages or more), you must break down your project into several components.

R & D (Research and Development): This is where we play Sherlock Holmes. Pertinent data is collected. We read and make notes. All serious **R & D** work begins at a good public library. Ask the librarian for *Bowker's Books in Print*, which lists all books available on your subject, or related subjects, by title, author and subject. If possible, check these books out. Many will be available at no cost from the library. Others can be purchased at bookstores, or directly from the publisher. Also ask the reference librarian for *Reader's Guide to Periodical Literature*, which lists magazine articles on almost every conceivable subject. Other good sources for information on a wide range of topics include the U.S. government. Write for the current catalog of "Select U.S. Government Publications (Superintendent of Documents, United States General Post Office, Box 1821, Washington, DC 20402). A Saturday afternoon can be well spent in one or more large used bookstores (found in all large cities and many small ones). There are great research treasures to be found in a used bookstore.

Select Your Chapters. By dividing your subject matter into chapters, you cut a full-blown book project down to manageable size. Sticking with our dream book concept, here are a few examples of logical chapter headings: *A History of Dream Analysis; The Secret of Capturing Your Dreams Before They Vanish; How to Understand Your*

Dreams; How to Give All of Your Dreams Happy Endings, etc. If we set up ten or twelve chapters (and we could have more or less), we reduce a full-size how-to project to the equivalent of ten or twelve magazine articles. And, that analogy fits well, for a *how-to* book is much like a series of magazine articles glued together. You'll also find it's so much simpler to do research, and add pieces of information to specific classifications (chapters) than to bring your writing and research to one major mountain, which is the whole book. Robert Schuller tells us *"inch by inch life's a cinch, but yard by yard, life is hard."* The same is true about writing books. Break your book project down to a chapter-by-chapter approach. It will make your task so much easier.

Once you have sufficient information for all the chapters you wish in your book, keeping in mind that it's all right for certain chapters to be much larger than others, it's now time to prepare your first draft, often called the "rough draft." By no means should you feel compelled to write your book page by page, chapter by chapter. Start anywhere you wish. Often it's a splendid idea to start with the chapter that interests you the most. Do anything to make your project a little joyful, instead of a Herculean ordeal.

Editing: When the first draft is finished, regardless of how rough and unconcise it may appear, it's time to add, delete and hone your manuscript, through the editing process. If you're not really a star editor type, and most of us aren't, hire someone who is. A journalism major at a local college is always eager to make some extra money. For a very reasonable fee—use $1.00 per page as a guide—he or she can help whip your manuscript into shape.

Ghost Writers: If you need lots of help to bring your book idea from conception to saleable (printed) state, you could hire a ghost writer to handle the entire project for you, or you could hire another writer to work side by side with you in the role of ghost co-writer and editorial assistant. Again, the cost for writing or editorial help is probably a lot less than you think. Good writers and editors come cheaply. I'm thankful I woke up years ago and realized that *the money is in the marketing and selling of books and information,* *not merely in writing and editing.* I recommend that you pay a flat fee for these services, and do not offer a royalty payment contract that will have these people sharing in book sale profits. Writing a book is hard work and takes some talent and determination. Selling a book at a profit takes a Master Marketing Genius. If you share profits with anyone, share with the man or woman who can successfully market!

Writing Style/ Use the K.I.S.S. (Keep it Simple, Stupid) approach. Don't try to impress your readers with ten-dollar words. Use the 25¢ words they understand (obviously, you may include professional jargon if your information package is targeted at scientists, doctors, lawyers, etc.). Short sentences and short paragraphs. Everything must flow, and be clear and concise. If it's easy to read and informs, you have done your job well.

PROTECT YOUR PROPERTY WITH A COPYRIGHT

Whatever you create on paper, be it a two-page "report" or a 2,000-page literary masterpiece, it is wise to protect your creative labor via the copyright method. This procedure is also simple and easy to obtain.

In 1976, after decades of confusion, the United States Congress updated copyright laws in this nation. Many new provisions were added, giving expanded protection to copyright holders.

Following is a brief, but hopefully, concise review of the new copyright law, plus information on how you can secure a copyright for everything you write.

WHAT IS A COPYRIGHT?

A copyright simply gives you the right to copy, distribute and sell an original work of authorship. It is a law protecting ownership. Generally, a person owns what he or she creates until he sells it, or assigns it to someone else, or until he or she accepts a salary for creating it (publishers often, but not always, hold the copyright). What we call copyright protection is the legal registration of that ownership. The copyright office, for a fee of $10, keeps a record of the date a property existed, to whom it belongs, and has on file in the Library of Congress two copies of the work. In cases of infringement litigation, these data are legal evidences that entitle the owner to obtain redress and collect damages. Copyright protection extends only to *works;* it does *not* extend to any idea, procedure, process, system, etc., regardless of the form in which it is described. That is, you can copyright sequences of words or sounds, of which a copy exists. You copyright the copy, not the content.

A person owns this right to copy only for a specific time. For works created after January 1, 1978, the new law provides a term lasting for the author's life, plus an additional 50 years after the author's death. For works made for hire, and for anonymous and pseudonymous works (unless the author's identity is revealed in Copyright Office records), the new terms will be 75 years from publication or 100 years from creation, whichever is shorter.

Under the old law, the term of copyright was 28 years, plus a second renewal term of 28 years, or 56 years in all. Under the new law, works in their first term must still be renewed, but they can be renewed for a term of 47 years, making a total of 75 years. Copyrights already in their second term at the time the new law went into effect are automatically extended up to the maximum of 75 years without the need for further renewal.

Among other featues, the new law also:
• incorporates into a single system proprietary copyright and what was formerly known as common-law copyright (ownership of unpublished works) and provides for the copyrighting of unpublished works;

• establishes guidelines for "fair use" for "purposes such as criticism, comment, news reporting, teaching, (including multiple choices for classroom use), scholarship, or research";

33

• creates a Copyright Royalty Tribunal which oversees royalty collections and payments to copyright owners for such uses as in jukeboxes, on public broadcasting, cable TV, etc.

WHAT CAN YOU COPYRIGHT?

Under the new Copyright Act, a claim of copyright is registered under a revised classification system. Instead of the fifteen classes provided under the old law, the new system provides for only five classes. Instead of the numerous application blanks and forms under the old law, the new law provides for only eight. They are:

1. CLASS TX: NON-DRAMATIC LITERARY WORKS. This category is very broad. Except for dramatic works and certain kinds of audiovisual works, Class TX includes all types of published and unpublished works written in words (or other verbal or numerical symbols), such as fiction, non-fiction, poetry, periodicals, textbooks, reference works, directories, catalogs, advertising copy, and the compilations of information.

To secure registration of copyright in this class, one uses application form TX, which replaces six old forms (Form A, Form A-B Foreign, Form A-B Ad Interim, Form B, Form BB, and Form C). You can obtain Form TX, or any copyright form you need, free of charge, by sending a specific request identifying the number of each form you need, to:

Copyright Office
Library of Congress
Washington, D.C. 20559

2. CLASS PA: WORKS OF THE PERFORMING ARTS. This category includes published and unpublished works prepared for the purpose of being performed directly before an audience or indirectly "by means of any device or process," such as radio or television. The category includes musical works, including any accompanying words; dramatic works, including any accompanying music; pantomimes and choreographic works; and motion pictures and other audiovisual works.

To register your copyright in this category use Form PA, which replaces four old forms (Form D, Form E, Form E-Foreign, and Form L-M).

CLASS VA: WORKS OF THE VISUAL ARTS. This category consists of published and unpublished works that are pictorial, graphic, and sculptural, including two-dimensional and three-dimensional works of fine, graphic, and applied art, photography, prints and art reproductions, maps, globes, charts, technical drawings, diagrams, and models.

If you wish to copyright a work of visual art, use Form VA, which replaces seven old forms (Form F, Form G, Form H, Form I, Form J, Form K, and Form KK).

4. CLASS SR: SOUND RECORDINGS. This category is appropriate for registration for both published and unpublished works in two situations: (1) where the copyright claim is limited to the recording itself; and (2) where the same copyright claimant is seeking to register not only the sound recording but also the musical, dramatic, or literary work embodied in the sound recording. With one exception, "sound recordings" are works that result from the fixation of a series of musical, spoken, or other sounds. This exception is for the audio portions of audiovisual works, such as motion picture soundtracks or audio cassettes accompanying a film strip; these are considered an integral part of the audiovisual work as a whole and must be registered in Class PA. Sound recordings made before February 15, 1972, are not eligible for registration, but may be protected by state law.

Use Form SR to register claim to a Sound Recording.

5. CLASS RE: RENEWAL REGISTRATION. This category is used for all renewals of copyrights that were in their first term when the new law went into effect. It covers renewals in all categories. Renewals can only be made in the 28th year of the first copyright registration and have the effect of extending copyright protection for an additional 47 years. Use Form RE for renewal registrations in all categories.

Under the new law, a genuine effort has been made to simplify the categories and red tape surrounding them, as can be seen by the one category/one form norm so far. However, the Copyright Office has found it necessary to create and use three other forms:

Use Form CA to apply for supplementary registration, to correct an error in a copyright registration, or to amplify the information given in a registration.

Use Form IS if you want to import copies of foreign edition of a non-dramatic literary work that is subject to the manufacturing requirements of section 601 of the new law, which requires with some exceptions and exemptions, that works copyrighted in the United States must be manufactured in the U.S. or Canada.

Use Form GR/CP (for group registration for contributions to periodicals) as an adjunct to a basic application on Form TX Form PA, or Form VA, if you are making a single registration for a group of works by the same individual author, all first published as contributions to periodicals within a twelve-month period, for example, a group of essays in a travel column, or a series of cartoons (cartoons would be registered in Class VA, visual arts), as provided in section 408(c)(2) of the new law.

In order to qualify for this registration, each contribution must have been published with a separate copyright notice in the name of the copyright owner. This is only a convenience for columnists who wish to register a collection of their work; it does not affect the ownership of the contributions, which belong to the author all along.

A writer does not lose his copyright in a work of authorship by virtue of its being published in a periodical. Article 201 (c), "Contributions to Collective Works," reads: "Copyright in each separate contribution to a collective work is distinct from copyright in the collective work as a whole, and vests initially in the author of the contribution. In the absence of an express transfer of the copyright or of any right under it, the owner of the copyright of the collective work is presumed to have acquired only the privilege of reproducing and distributing the contribution as part of that collective work, any revision of that collective work, and any later collective work in the same series." In other words, unless you agree to something different, a magazine acquires only one-time rights when it publishes a story or article.

STEP-BY-STEP

To secure copyright for a published, non-dramatic, literary work, here is what you must do:

First: Publish the work *with the copyright notice.* The law requires that a copyright notice in a specified form "shall be placed on all publicly distributed copies" of the work, on the title page, or (more commonly) on the back side of the title page, or as part of the colophon in a magazine. Use of the copyright notice consists of three elements: (1) the symbol "©", or the word "Copyright," or the abbreviation "Copr."; (2) the year of the first publication; and (3) the name of the copyright owner. For example: "Copyright 1987, Profit Ideas." (Copyrights can be a person's name or a company's name.)

Unlike the old law, the new law provides procedures for correcting errors in the copyright notice, and even for curing the omission of the notice altogether. However, failure to comply with the requirement for copyright notice correctly may result in loss of some areas of valuable copyright protection. If not corrected within five years, you can blow your entire copyright.

Second: Fill out the proper application forms. For a non-dramatic literary work, the proper form would be Form TX. Write the Copyright Office for the blanks, then fill them out carefully, using a typewriter or dark ink, after reading the instructions.

Third: Send the required fee, the required copies, and the completed application to "The Registrar of Copyrights,

Library of Congress, Washington, D.C. 20559." The fee for a first copyright of a book is now $10, which must be paid by check or money order made payable to "The Registrar of Copyrights." You are required to deposit two copies of the published work with the Library of Congress (one copy of unpublished works and one copy of contributions to collective works). These are the copies that become evidence in infringement litigation. Send the fee, the copies, and the application together.

When the Registrar of Copyrights has processed your application and filed the copies, you will receive an official certificate of copyright, bearing the official seal of the Copyright Office. That certificate is your evidence of ownership.

Surprising as it may seem, many self-publishers never bother to copyright their work. This is often the case with publishers of small booklets, reports, etc., while some small publishers seem to worry too much about someone "stealing" their precious literary creations. Others seem to worry, not at all, and don't ever bother to copyright.

While it's unlikely another will knock off your information book, manual, etc., word for word, and there is little you can do about them stealing ideas of yours, it's still a good idea to copyright everything you write and publish.

HOW TO START
YOUR OWN COMPANY

Setting yourself up in business is not as difficult as many think it will be. While there are no unusual legal requirements to sell books and other "paper and ink" products, or audio/visual items, by mail, you *do* need to follow sound business guidelines.

Once you have decided to go into the information-by-mail business, you must turn your attention to some of the practical questions related to starting any business: *How should I structure my new business* (sole proprietorship, partnership, or corporation). *Do I have enough money to get my new venture off the ground, or will I have to raise more capital from other sources?*

Let's look at each of these methods.

SOLE PROPRIETORSHIP

This is the fastest way to open a business. You simply use your own name or register a fictitious name, and you're in business. Most entrepreneurs who enter the information-by-mail business do so as a sole or single proprietor. Some remain as single proprietors, others incorporate at a later date, when profits become substantial.

OBTAINING A D.B.A.
AND/OR A BUSINESS LICENSE

In most cities and towns, you will need a "d.b.a." (doing business as) if you use a name other than your own. Also, most municipalities require all types of businesses to be licensed. The cost is almost always very modest and the procedure is a simple one. Call your local city or county clerk's office to obtain details on exactly what is required in your area.

A BUSINESS CHECKING ACCOUNT

Once you establish your d.b.a. and secure a business license (if one is required in your locality), it's time to open your business checking account. In the mail bookselling business you will soon be depositing a large number of checks and money orders. If there are several banks in your area, take some time to check them out individually. You are looking for one that charges the lowest service charges, charge per check written, etc. All banks are not the same. Comparison shopping could save you $100 or even more per year in banking fees.

You may also want to inquire about getting a credit card in your company name and/or attempt to secure a Visa/Mastercard arrangement so that you can accept credit card purchases from your mail order book-buying customers. Often, a banker is somewhat reluctant to set you up with credit card privileges when you first start a new business. However, once you establish your company with the bank (6 to 12 months may be required to do this), they often become more cooperative.

PARTNERSHIPS

If you lack necessary capital to launch your business on your own (how much capital you need will be covered later), you may wish to go into business with someone else, although there are negative as well as positive reasons in forming a partnership. Sharing profits and the difficulty people have in enjoying a suitable (compatible) partnership, are two major drawbacks.

CORPORATION

A corporation is an entity who continues to exist. It is easily transferable and can have considerable tax advantages once you begin doing substantial business ($250,000 or more annually). Increased regulations, detailed record keeping, and the initial incorporation fees are major drawbacks.

YOUR PLACE OF BUSINESS

You can conduct business from your home or you can rent office space. To conserve money, it is wise to start right at home. Fact is, many veteran information by mail sellers continue to do business in their homes, even after achieving great success. This is the age of information, and it's also a fact—more and more people are discovering the many advantages of living and working in the same place—home, sweet home.

In the beginning, you won't need a lot of space to launch your business. Later, when more room is needed, you'll have to either rent office and warehouse space, or if you prefer to continue to do business from your home, you can rent mini-

WHAT FORM OF
BUSINESS ORGANIZATION?

SINGLE PROPRIETORSHIP

ADVANTAGES

1. Low start-up costs
2. Greatest freedom from regulation
3. Owner in direct control
4. Minimal working capital
   Tax advantage to small owner
6. All profits to owner

DISADVANTAGES

1. Greater liability
2. Lack of continuity
3. More difficult to raise capital

PARTNERSHIP

ADVANTAGES

1. Ease of formation
2. Low start-up costs
3. Additional sources of venture capital
4. Broader management base
5. Possible tax advantage
6. Limited outside regulation

DISADVANTAGES

1. Unlimited liability
2. Lack of continuity
3. Divided authority
4. Difficulty in raising additional capital
5. Hard to find suitable partners
6. Divided profits

CORPORATION

ADVANTAGES

1. Limited liability
2. Specialized management
3. Ownership is transferable
4. Continuous existence
5. Legal entity
5. Possible tax advantages
6. Easier to raise capital

DISADVANTAGES

1. Closely regulated
2. Most expensive form to organize
3. Charter restrictions
4. More record-keeping necessary
5. Double taxation
6. More initial money required to incorporate

storage space at one of the thousands of self-contained storage rental centers that are now found almost everywhere.

Your mailing address can be your home address, a post office box, or a private mail drop. (Thousands of private mail centers have opened in recent years, and they offer entrepreneurs a choice between using their home address (not too good an idea in an all residential area, especially if you don't want potential local customers knocking on your door), and a post office box (there are still some people who believe a street address adds more stability than a postal box). Many of the private mail centers will let you use their street address and then assign you a box number to go with it. In some cases, you can substitute a "Suite" number for the box number.

Listed below are examples of all three options, and how they'll look. You decide which one you like.

Information Marketing Services
120 Elm Street
Your city, state and zip

Information Marketing Services
P.O. Box 280
Your city, state, zip

Information Marketing Services
850 Market St., Suite 307,
Your city, state, zip

Obviously, your home address will add no extra cost. A post office box is most reasonable, from $20 to $50 per year, according to the size of the box rented. A private mail center will cost considerably more. At between $10 and $18 per month, on the average, your yearly rate will be in the $120 to $200 range.

CHOOSE YOUR COMPANY NAME
WITH INSIGHT

The name you hang on your new information sales business can create a positive or negative image.

Don't choose your new company name in a haphazard fashion. The name you give to your new fledgling firm could be a liability or an asset. It can help entice orders or turn potential customers off.

Many new business people simply use their own name. If it is your name, it need not be registered, which is required by most states when fictitious names are used. Although this practice works for some, often it is wiser to use a company name that is either catchy or gives a better description of the products you sell. A good company name will also enhance your presence and create the illusion of strength and stability.

The late mail order genius, Joe Karbo, earned millions using his own name to sell his famous classic "The Lazy Man's Way to Riches." Using his own name fit perfectly with the kick-back "Lazy Joe" image his ad copy was conveying. Ben Suarez took just the opposite approach in his road to fortune. Selling books from his own home, he gave his new company a grand name—The Publishing Corporation of America! And when he was selling over a million of his "Life-Luck Horoscopes," he created the perfect name to market the horoscopes—The International Astrological Association. Now, think about it! Wouldn't you feel better about ordering astrology items from The International Astrological Association than in placing your order to just a person's name? Keep this in mind when you pick a name to do business with. In some cases, your own name may do fine; in others, you can give yourself a powerful image by selecting a name that fits your particular field of information, or is just a good, solid name that is easy to remember.

Personally, I like names that give me some flexibility, but which are also solid names. In addition to using my own name, here are some company names I have owned or have been affiliated with (many of them are still very, very active).

Advance Sales Corp.
American Amusement Company
50,000 Books
I Am Curious Book Company

Independent Publishers Network
Profit Ideas
Publishers Media

Overall, I think they are good, solid names, and yet a multitude of different books, products and services could be sold under the banner of each.

I like to have such creative options. I knew a company in Boston that specialized in cookbook publishing and called itself *The Boston Baking and Publishing Company.* When they decided to expand, diversify and publish new books and booklets on herbs, organic gardening, etc., they had an identity crisis and had to hunt for a new name.

Unless you are quite certain you will hold forth in one specialized area (and that may not be a bad idea), give yourself a company name that gives you lots of latitude to sell books, reports, or other information-by-mail products that cross categorical lines.

YOUR LOGO

While some logos are nothing more than a "ridiculous riddle" (I'm talking about those that use ultra-modern graphics that are not readily understandable), others are simple, direct and do have impact. Don't be dumb, or go on an ego trip. If you use a logo, use the K.I.S.S. approach. Make sure it fits your name and image. What could be more simple and direct than the Profit Ideas logo?

PRESENT AN IMPRESSIVE IMAGE

Don't make the mistake of announcing to the world, "I'm a mail order beginner!" Honesty and modesty are admirable traits, but don't mistake a bad business attitude and poor image for openness.

Your customers will be asked to order information by mail that they know very little about from a company they know nothing about. That's a tall order, and you can't blame them for being more than a little skeptical. The more skeptical they become, the less likely they favor you with their order.

One professional method to help build confidence is to produce professional-appearing advertising and sales material. Also, quality letterheads and envelopes are a must! Do all you can to convey an impressive businesslike image. Quality printed matter and well-designed ads cost only slightly more than pathetic promotional material and sloppy sales literature. Too often the money you save on slipshod printing and advertising is lost many times over on lost sales.

In mail order selling, your stationery and literature is you! Without spending a fortune, strive to create a positive image. Never, but never, use sloppy stationery, envelopes or flyers that are poorly printed, messy rubber stamps, etc. Before you seal your envelope, carefully consider its content. What statement are you making about yourself and your business?

GETTING STARTED FROM SCRATCH

A home-based mail order business can literally be started from the kitchen table. Many operators started in just that way, before proceeding to "more businesslike quarters" in the home or an outside office.

When the kitchen table offers the only necessary space, use it. However, if at all possible, search out other areas of your house or apartment that offer more privacy. Your own home office or a spare bedroom that can be converted to office space is ideal. Even open space in a garage may serve your initial startup needs.

BASIC SUPPLIES AND EQUIPMENT

(1) a desk and chair
(2) file cabinet
(3) envelopes and letterheads
(4) typewriter
(5) storage area/folding table
(6) miscellaneous office supplies (rubber bands, paper clips, envelope openers, glue, typewriter correction liquid, etc.)
(7) a large wastebasket
(8) proper lighting
(9) postage stamps
(10) checking account
(11) a bookkeeping system

You may, of course, improvise. Any table, including the kitchen table, may serve as your desk during your initial start. However, do get yourself a desk, even if it is a used one from the Goodwill or Salvation Army, as soon as you can. Your own desk will give you a more positive feeling of "being in business for yourself." Likewise, you could use a spare closet or your own bookshelves in place of a file cabinet at first, but again, purchase a sturdy four-drawer file cabinet as soon as possible.

It is almost impossible to do business without using a typewriter. You can either buy one second-hand or rent a nice model by the month at reasonable rates. If you can't even "two-finger type," a typing course at a local adult education school should have you pecking away in good order, and these classes usually charge very low tuition. If you are married or live with someone with office skills, they can be of real help to you.

You need storage space to keep the items you intend to sell by mail. And the other items on my list (envelopes, stamps, office supplies, etc.) are essential to any kind of mail order business.

Don't underestimate the importance of adequate lighting. Also, purchase a large comprehensive journal at an office supply store and get started right by keeping good business records. Your record-keeping is vital. It will tell you in which direction your business is heading. A separate checking account for your mail order business is important. Make notations as to what every check went for (supplies, advertising, rentals, etc.) and this will assist you in keeping good records. More on this a little later.

You also need a phone on or near your desk or work area. It may be called the mail order business, yet you will still find yourself using the telephone often to order supplies, obtain information, etc. You may or may not wish to use your own phone number in your ads, catalogs and circulars going to your customers. Some mail order companies do, with satisfactory results; others prefer that all business be done by mail.

AFFILIATIONS FOR CREDIBILITY AND ASSISTANCE

To add more credibility to your new venture, you should consider joining the following:

► The Better Business Bureau of your area
► The local Chamber of Commerce
► The Independent Publishers Network (IPN)
► The American Bookdealers Exchange (ABE)

Both the IPN and the ABE (addresses in the *Source Directory section of this book)*, are progressive marketing information organizations for independent publishers and mail order information sellers.

GOOD RECORD-KEEPING IS ESSENTIAL

Record-keeping is boring. It also is vital. If you can't stand the thought of keeping records, you will have to pay for the services of a bookkeeper—for many of us, a smart idea. However, in the early stages of operating your new business, you probably will want to conserve your money. If hiring the services of a bookkeeper sounds like an unnecessary luxury, do yourself a service, and start keeping records of all your buy-sell transactions.

47

Start right and stick with it. Purchase a full-size ledger at a local office supply (or from one of the mail order stationery firms in my *Source* section). Label the columns on the expense side as follows:

(1) Advertising
(2) Postage and mailing
(3) Supplies for resale
(4) All other supplies
(5) Telephone
(6) Utilities
(7) Travel
(8) Meals and lodging
(9) Auto expenses
(10) Rent/mortgage
(11) Business books, magazines/newsletter subscriptions
(12) Entertainment
(13) Leased or purchased equipment
(14) Licenses and permits
(15) Refunds
(16) Bookkeeping, banking, accounting, legal
(17) Miscellaneous

Although the above 17 categories are general, they apply to most mail order operations. In time, you may wish to add a category or two that you find to be singularly important to your business.

THE NOT RECOMMENDED
(BUT IT DOES WORK)
ONCE-A-YEAR METHOD
OF RECORD-KEEPING

Up until the time I hired a bookkeeper, this was the only way I wanted to deal with records:

As Easy as One, Two, Three...

(1) A big cardboard box is propped up on a top shelf in the office.

(2) Every single paid bill was dated, marked and coded as

per the 17 categories just mentioned. A brief description was also added, and the method of payment (credit card, cash or check). Next the paid bill was unceremoniously tossed into the big cardboard box.

(3) On Super Bowl Sunday (a magnificent Sunday in mid to late January) I experienced a *blessing* and a *curse*: The *blessing* was the Super Bowl football game; the *Curse* was I put the previous years records in order. The game lasts a little more than three afternoon hours; the record-sorting and ledgering can keep you going till midnight. Of course there is a better way, such as updating your ledger on either a weekly or monthly basis. However, for some of us, the once a year ordeal *does* work.

Obviously, it's vital you know which direction your business is heading. Good weekly or monthly record-keeping will tell you this. However, for once-a-year record dodgers, paying almost every bill from one checking account or a combination of checks from one account plus one credit card used only for business, you should know just about where you're at and where you're going.

YOU AND THE LAW

While there are not many particular or unusual laws that govern the mail order information selling business, there are three important laws that must be adhered to:

(1) All orders must be shipped within 30 days of receipt, or the customer made aware of the added anticipated delay, while being given the option to get his or her money back (*here at Profit Ideas it has always been our policy to ship our orders and our dealer dropship orders the same day they are received*).

(2) The book or other information product you send to your customer must be similar to that which was described in your ad or mailing literature.

(3) Unless you state that you offer no moneyback guarantee (and that tactic will reduce your orders!), you must return

a customer's money if he or she returns the product (book) in reasonably good shape within 60 days or less. You can check with your local Better Business Bureau (BBB) and/or Chamber of Commerce concerning other general business rules and regulations.

Chapter 3

OPERATING YOUR BUSINESS

Operating a mail order information business from your home or rented office, requires that you set up *policies and procedures* that will allow your business to run as smoothly as possible. Here are some ideas to consider when setting policy on...

Accounts Payable: While many mail order operators only sell C.W.O. (Cash With Order), others sell C.W.O., C.O.D., open account to the buyer retail, and/or open account to other dealers, wholesale.

While C.W.O. (this can mean cash, check, moneyorder or credit card order) is definitely the most desirable sale, in that you are paid before you ship, many dealers are willing to take calculated risks of being paid at a future date (after shipping the order) for various reasons, namely: (A) the privilege of placing an order without advance payment will always increase the number of orders from mail order book information buyers; (B) wholesale dealers, especially the bigger ones, often require open account shipping and terms of 30, 60, or even 90 days. In the case of some mail trade distributors and book trade distributors, not only is open account shipping requested, but certain companies even expect a form of consignment billing, where you, as the prime source (be you the publisher or source distributor) only get paid after your items sell. A good deal for them, not too good for you.

My policy, which has evolved over 20 years in this crazy, yet wonderful business is this: I always require payment in advance from consumers. I always require payment in advance, with appropriate discounts, to relatively small wholesalers and distributors. I will only ship open account to large wholesale/distributor sources who are well established and stable, and then only when a detailed payment policy has been approved and a contract signed. I always seek out and encourage "pay first" deals.

To entice even the larger wholesale accounts to pay in advance, I have found it advantageous to offer deeper discounts. The old cliche, *A bird in the hand is better than two in the bush,* still rings true!

I'd much rather sell 200 copies of books, manuals, directories, etc., at a large discount, let's say 70% off retail, than to sell 400 copies at only 60% off retail with terms that give the wholesale buyer the right to pay only after sales are made, plus the right to return unsold copies. I hate such terms! *Take the cash and let the credit go!*

Open Account Shipping to Single Copy Buyers: It's a fact, you will receive many more orders (often twice as many, or even far more than that) when you allow information buyers to look before they pay. Leading publishers like Prentice-Hall, and all of the major book clubs, do business this way. On the plus side, you'll dramatically increase your orders; on the minus side, you'll create a paperwork/billing mountain for yourself. From 20% to 40% of the people who order (depending on where you place your ads or which mailing lists you use) will never pay for the books they receive. Not ever. In addition, your returns will at least quadruple. If 2% of your C.W.O. buyers return their purchase for a refund, no less than 8%, and quite likely 10% or more, will return the *review* copies to you. Most likely, on all ad or mailing campaigns which feature *review before pay* privileges, you will eventually receive payment from only 55% to 75% of all responders. And, only after invoices, statements, and several follow-up "payment requested" mailings.

To run a successful "pay only after review" operation, you must meet three important criteria:

(1) You must test-test-test and convince yourself the "bottom line" is covered with black ink.

(2) You must set yourself up to handle the massive amount of paperwork that will be required.

(3) You will need to possess a strong stomach and a sound nervous system (by this I mean, you must cope with, and psychologically handle, the fact that a large number of responders will request, read, keep, but never ever pay for your printed product. In effect: *Thanks for the free book, chump.*

Most "open account shipping" operators hook up with a collection agency as the last resort to try to obtain payment. But even then, many won't pay, and on those who *do* pay through the agency, you will only obtain a percentage of the money received. On small debts, many collection agencies require up to half of all money they collect.

Thanks, but no thanks! I don't want all these headaches. We don't ship open account to mail order buyers. I don't even offer C.O.D. ordering. However, some dealers who are willing to handle all the paper, and all the hassles, have made *look first—pay later* mail order a success.

Pricing: Correct pricing of your paper and ink products is vital to your success. On your *mainline products* you need markups of at least two times cost (and the higher, the better). An item that sells for $29.95 must cost you $9.95 or less to buy or to print. The only two exceptions would be (1) if you offer a "catalog" of many items that encourages multiple sales, or (2) those items that you use for follow-up or "bounce back" sales. Even on items purchased from other sources for follow-up mailings to proven buyers or bounce-backers (package stuffers sent with orders), you should never offer anything that does not allow you a 100% markup. Always at least double your money, or forget it!

While a minimum 2 to 1 markup is absolutely essential, many mail order information peddlers strive for markup in the 5 to 1—10 to 1 range. They believe more is better, and for good reasons: the cost of your printed product will never be your chief expense. Advertising, postage and mailing costs will always head the list of primary expenses.

Over the years I have discovered the following breakdown on percentages of the expense dollar:

Ads, postage/mailing 51%
Printing & product purchasing 22%
Help—both inside & outside* 9%
Space and equipment rentals 8%
All other expenses 10%

MAIL HANDLING PROCEDURES

The morning mail should be picked up early if you receive it from a rented post office box. If you have it delivered to your home or office address, you are at the mercy of your mail carrier. In either case, here is a method that you, your spouse or someone who works for you can use to handle the day's mail.

(1) Open all mail.

(2) Sort mail into piles of (A) orders; (B) inquiries; (C) bills; (D) advertising and (E) "white mail."

Let me digress to make sure you understand the five categories. Orders and/or standard inquiries would be response

---

*In the information by mail business you can get started without any hired help, but as you grow larger you will probably require either inside help (people who will probably work exclusively for you) or outside help (independent contractors who perform certain tasks for you on a pay-by-performance basis). All creative services you obtain—copywriting, graphic artists, typing, typesetting, etc., can be considered outside help.

from direct mailings or space ads. Bills would be invoices to you from suppliers, equipment rental firms, utility companies, etc. Advertising is offers sent you from other mail order dealers. "White mail" is letters from buyers or inquiries that require personal attention and a specific answer not found in your regular sales literature.

(3) Type labels from orders and/or inquiries. Use multiple carbon sheets and "key" each label so that you know exactly what was ordered and the date.

Example:

122086-TS
Susan Criswall
110 Palm Blvd.
El Cajon, CA 92022

This would tell me that on December 20, 1986, Susan Criswall ordered my book, *How to Achieve Total Success.*

(4) Place labels and postage on orders and inquiry envelopes. To "stay ahead" of your incoming mail, it is wise to pre-package orders and inquiry mail. In this way it is ready for postage and labeling and fast turnaround. Don't forget to enclose circulars or catalogs to get those *bounce-back* orders.

(5) Place the extra carbon copies of the labels on index cards and file (in the case of a two-step inquiry ad program, you may wish to set up a follow-up system). Let's say your program required three follow-ups after the original mailing, spaced 14 days apart. Using two file folders to cover a two-month span can accomplish this. If an inquiry is received, let's say, July 14, then we would include a July 28 label in our July folder and two labels (8/11 and 8/25) in the August folder.

(6) Take care of your "white mail" by answering questions, settling complaints, etc. "White Mail" means special requests, inquiries about orders, or any correspondence that cannot be answered by sending a printed matter.

(7) Go through the advertising you received. Handle and release everything in one of three ways: (A) place an order for something you want or need that will help your business, (B) file for future reference (supply catalogs, etc.), or (C) throw it away.

Anyone in mail order selling for any length of time knows it is all too easy to get bogged down with stacks of mail. This can create a real problem. To avoid getting behind on your business mail, take care of your mail handling responsibilities daily.

You can lose valuable repeat business by taking too long to fill orders or inquiries (a 48-hour or less turnaround is good business practice), and you can even get yourself into hot water with the post office and other consumer agencies if you're extremely tardy in filling orders. The law now requires that all orders be filled within 30 days or the customer be sent an explanation as to when it will be filled, along with the option for the customer to get a full refund if he or she does not want to wait any longer.

ADDRESSING SYSTEMS

If you plan to stay in contact with your customers with regular follow-up mailings, as most established dealers do, or wish to rent your mailing lists, you need an addressing system. Here are your options:

Computer Controlled System. Your mailing list is key punched on computer card stock and entered into a computer retrieval system. Your computer company can then give you a printout by states or sectional center breakdown on paper, cheshire labels, gummed labels or magnetic tape. This system is probably the best way to go when you have a large mailing list.

Scriptomatic Systems. This system places a coating of special carbon on card stock. Each time the card is used, a little amount of the carbon is applied to an envelope. The carbon addressing part of the card is on the top of each card and there is plenty of room below for you to log orders or inquir-

56

ies in pencil or pen. Thus, this system serves a dual purpose—
(A) it is a rapid mailing vehicle and (B) it is a record-keeping
system.

Addressograph System. Here metal plates are used that require machine cutting. The advantage here is that, although more costly, these plates will last indefinitely, whereas the Scriptomatic System and other "paper plate" type systems must be replaced every few years.

SHIPPING ORDERS

It is very important that all orders be quickly processed and shipped. Every day an order is delayed, the probability of complaints, cancellations and returns increases. It is often wise to send a postcard the day the order comes in, telling the customer that the order has been received and that it is being sent by parcel post or UPS. This should always be done on big ticket orders, or for any order that can't be shipped promptly.

If you're shipping something that is quite heavy and bulky, UPS is often a better choice than the post office.

STAY FRIENDLY WITH
YOUR LOCAL POST OFFICE

It will pay you real dividends to have an amicable relationship with everyone who works at your local post office.

Although postal workers are supposed to treat everyone impartially, I have seen "preferred service" given to customers well-liked by postal employees. Yours truly, on occasion, has enjoyed a little extra service, which I sincerely appreciate.

USE A MONEY-BACK GUARANTEE

Mail order customers expect you to offer a guarantee. For most dealers, overall returned merchandise is quite low. Nevertheless, a Money Back Guarantee is of real importance.

It instills confidence in the potential buyer. It tells him or her that you aim to please and that you won't take the money and run. A 30-day return guarantee is most often used by mail order dealers, but even a short 10-day guarantee is far better than no guarantee.

In recent years, several large mail dealers have begun to employ a very special guarantee whereby the customer's check or money order is held uncashed for 30 days. Joe Karbo, a very innovative bookseller, originated this unique guarantee enroute to earning millions on a very popular book titled *The Lazy Man's Way to Riches*. In recent years dozens of others have copied this approach. Joe was a real pro and a true genius in selling books by mail. Still, I do not recommend this approach for the just-getting-started-in-mail-order entrepreneur. In the early stages of mail selling, your cash flow is going to be vital and you'll probably need to bank every dollar the same day it arrives at your home, office or post office box.

MAKE IT EASY TO ORDER

While the personal or business check is still the most popular vehicle of ordering, the sharp entrepreneur makes it easy to order. We accept checks, money orders, Visa, Master Card or cash. I suggest you do likewise.

TELEPHONE ORDERS

Between 10% and 50% of all orders received by many mail order firms are obtained by using a toll-free 800 number. Once you have your business moving, even if only a part-time start, you owe it to yourself to at least consider renting an 800 service from a telephone marketing company. At the very least, you should use your own telephone number on your ads, letters and circulars, especially if you have back-up offers that will benefit from personalized explanation.

Several of the leading mail order book, newsletter and magazine publishers (KCI Communications, Howard J. Ruff, etc.) have set up elaborate telephone systems to assist their subscribers and buyers with various business opportunities, investment information, etc. Many sharp dealers offer this service "free." As an exciting and profitable result of their "free services," they often sell the caller additional plans, books and subscriptions. They enjoy the best of two worlds—(A) they provide a much-appreciated service and (B) they often turn public service into personal profit.

SELL THROUGH OTHER DEALERS

When you have an information product that is under your control (you're either the publisher or you have some kind of mail order exclusive), you may wish to consider selling wholesale to other mail order dealers. True, you will have to sell at a much lower price per unit than direct to customers; nevertheless, ad costs are usually greatly reduced also. Many established firms earn either (A) their chief revenue or (B) substantial additional revenues in selling products to other dealers, inside or outside the mail trade. As I mentioned earlier, consider offering substantial discounts, while obtaining C.W.O.

MORE ABOUT
DROP-SHIP SELLING

In addition to, or in place of selling your products or services to other agents and dealers for their resale, you may want to consider drop ship mail order selling.

You may wish to use drop-ship selling on both ends—(A) making your products available to others via drop shipping or (B) offering similar items to what you're now selling that can be drop-shipped for you by other sources of supply.

The beauty of drop-shipping is, with the exception of sales literature or ads, no money is tied up in merchandise. Drop ship items are placed in ads or in direct mailings. When orders arrive, the dealer subtracts his "commission" (usually ½ the money received) and then sends the order on with a completed shipping label for the prime source to fill and ship.

While I never recommend drop shipping as a main source of your mail order income, I do think it is wise to either order and sell, or sell via drop shipping, information products and services that complement your main offer.

For example, some dealers ship orders to customers without any sales literature enclosed. I strongly recommend including several circulars, etc., as package inserts on all orders you fill. These backup offers can be for items that other dealers will drop-ship for you. They can produce many easy "bounce-back" orders that cost you very little to obtain.

Offering your printed products to other dealers to sell through drop-shipping can also reap you many cost-effective orders. You ought to have a high enough markup built into your offers that by accepting ½-off retail prices you still greatly prosper.

DO EVERYTHING TO PLEASE YOUR CUSTOMERS

To win success in mail order you must do everything possible to please your mail customers.

I have already mentioned the importance of handling orders, inquiries and "white mail" as quickly as possible. Most mail order entrepreneurs do a reasonably good job at processing and mailing orders and inquiries. It is the special request letters, some of which are long and tedious, and various complaints or misunderstandings that too often pile up unanswered. While I strongly urge you to send off orders or inquiries in 48 hours or less, you may take a little longer to respond to your unclassified mail, which I call "white mail."

Some mail dealers have found it works well to set aside a specific time each week (it could be Monday mornings or Friday afternoons) to get completely caught up with all white mail received the previous week. However you decide to handle your white mail, just make certain you take care of it on a regular basis. Nothing less than at least once a week will do, and in case of urgent requests for personalized information or a very irate complaint, it should be taken care of without any delay.

Satisfied customers are the rockbed foundation on which mail order fortunes are built. Keep them happy and they will keep sending in their orders. And repeat business is a major factor in achieving mail order success.

"Never give your customers their moneysworth—give them much more than their moneysworth. They'll love you for it and reward you with more business."

RvH

Chapter 4

SPECIALIZE YOUR MAIL ORDER VENTURE—OFFER "RELATED INFORMATION"

Only a handful of major corporations who publish full-size hardbound and paperback books, have been successful with a long line of unrelated titles. For most publishing companies, specialization is the key to profits.

As a new self-publisher and/or mail book-seller, you should structure your operation to offering select groups of related information—books, booklets, directories, reports, etc. You may be anxious to try several different kinds of items at once, but please don't! Diversification will drain your resources, and also force you to develop more than one marketing plan. Far too risky for the new information seller or anyone who wants to quickly establish a profit center.

HOW TO SELECT YOUR PRODUCTS

Nearly all of the successful mail order information sellers I know, including myself, use this two-step approach in deciding what they will sell:

(1) Sell information you already have inside your head, or

(2) Sell information that interests you, and which you are most willing, and able, to research, find, develop and/or purchase for sale.

I've found that a person always will achieve more in a field he knows well and/or likes. Thus, you'll do well to apply the above criteria in deciding what type of *paper and ink information* you will sell. Sure, you can get involved in a new topic area—*any* topic area in fact—but it should be a field that gets your juices flowing. And one that you're anxious to dig into and develop some expertise in.

WHAT SELLS BEST?

A difficult question to answer, because so many different specialization topics can be turned into great moneymaking ventures. In 20 years of information-by-mail selling, I have personally known individuals who have become very rich (million dollar rich!) offering the following types of information. From A to Z, here's a partial list:

Astrology and occult; all types of business books and reports, including how to start a business; casino gambling; cookbooks; fishing and hunting; health and diet plans; horse racing tips; import/export guides; lottery playing instructions; mailing lists of all kinds, including specialized industry name and address directories; many different real estate investment books, manuals and tapes; stock market guides and newsletters; sexual instructions of all types; and sources-of-supply directories.

While there are hundreds of other types of information products that people are selling and prospering with, I think you'll have to agree, my own little list is far-ranging. It proves that a wide variety of subject matter is in demand, and can be packaged, printed and sold for huge profits by mail.

Pick your subject matter and know that you can be successful. Also, build a related line of information products, so that you can receive many "bounce-back" and follow-up orders.

You may have to begin with one item that you package and self-publish. However, it's good biz to seek out closely related items that you can also publish or buy for resale. This will greatly increase your sales volume and bottom line, with the exception of a few "high ticket" items that can be sold for $100 or more retail, it's impossible to be very successful as a one-item-only mail dealer.

CATALOGS FOR SUCCESS

There is a fortune to be made by developing your own catalog of related items to sell by mail. A catalog can transform a one-shot buyer into a multiple buyer, thus substantially increasing your gross and net profits. While it may be impossible for you to develop your own catalog in the very beginning of your new venture, catalog development should be both your short-range and long-range goal. I say short and long range because catalogs can be small and simple, or big and elaborate. Perhaps when you hear the word catalog, you immediately conjure up the image of one of the big and beautiful colorful books produced by major mail order companies such as *The Sharper Image* or *JS&A Products that Think*. Yes, these are fine mail order catalogs, but you can have your own simple catalog that is smaller and less colorful, yet still very effective.

By giving your catalog (and it can be as simple as an 11x17" brochure, printed on both sides, and folded to make four 8½x11 pages) a good, solid title and a strong theme, it can produce desired results. You also don't need hundreds of items in your catalog, although you will want to feature at least a half dozen, and if possible, more.

If you have self-published only one or two books, manuals or reports, you will want to highlight these items that you control, giving them a good amount of space. Other items in your catalog could come from other supply sources, which, while somewhat different than your items, nevertheless compliment and are related, and thus likely to be of interest to the person who is interested in your specialized line.

If finances permit, typeset your catalog, using a few strong graphics for illustration purposes. However, even a plain, typewritten catalog, if the title and theme demand attention, can be a great sales tool.

Your catalog should be updated regularly, hopefully getting bigger and better each time. Publishing a catalog quarterly, with new items added each time you print, is recommended. You must keep mailing to all previous buyers, and at least four mailings per year to your own customer mailing list is essential.

As your catalog grows in size and substance, you will also be able to do some test mailings to rented lists of buyers of information similar to what you sell.

Caution: You may be tempted to make your early catalogs into self-mailers to save envelope costs. Don't do it! While some big, beautiful catalogs do work as self-mailers, smaller, less elaborate ones usually do not. The smaller and less artistically prestigious your catalog is, the more you need an envelope to send it in, and above all else, a powerful sales letter to put your prospective buyer in *the right mood* before he or she begins to look at your catalog.

Regardless of how small and/or plain your own first catalogs are, make certain they are crisp, appealing, and punchy. Black ink on white paper is too bland. You're not selling *vanilla*! Black ink on a color paper stock (I like the earth tones, goldenrod, buff, salmon and canary) will give it some pizazz.

A two-color job (and black and red ink on white or yellow paper sparkles) can bring your catalog to life. Your sales letter is a different story. Simple black and white here almost always works best.

The six most important factors to consider when sending out a small and/or graphically plain catalog are:

(1) your sales letter
(2) the title of your catalog
(3) the theme of the catalog
(4) the appearance of the catalog
(5) your order form (make it easy to use)
(6) enclosure of a return envelope

Your sales letter, when sent with a smaller or less elaborate catalog, should be separate. Do not print it as page one or page two in the catalog itself. Your order form can also be separate, but it's okay for it to be printed within the catalog. A separate order form often pulls better than a printed within one, but it may not pull enough extra to warrant the additional printing cost. Only individual testing will reveal that answer for you.

Effective catalogs often separate the mail order winners from the mail order losers. Start thinking about producing yours!

You really can make a fortune selling information by mail, but to do just that, you must always be thinking about maximizing your gross and profits, while holding the lid down on expenses.

PAY FOR SERVICE— NOT FOR TIME

One of the best ways for a mail order dealer to keep costs in line is to rely on "outside help" (independent contractors) to provide most or all of the special services (copy, art, typing, stuffing, big mailings, etc.) that you require. I believe these people should be paid by the job, not by the hour. Example: some time ago we asked two different home typists (we always cultivate and have on file a list of home workers) to look up and type out names and addresses from various directories. One lady was paid 4 cents each (which she considered fair) for every name and address she typed; the other was paid a straight $4.50 per hour for the same service. Each returned in a week having typed 2,500 names and addresses. $100 was paid to lady No. 1 for services rendered. Lady No. 2, who also typed 2,500 names and addresses, submitted her bill for 39 hours, at $4.50 per hour. Total: $166.50 for her service.

Obviously a home typing service is a low end expense. Not so with copywriters and graphic artists. A friend in Los Angeles who sells books by mail, recently told me that he hired a graphic artist to design his catalog. She told him she could estimate the job and give him a flat rate of $600, or he could pay her for actual hours worked at $35 per hour. Since he didn't think the job would be too time-consuming, he opted for the hourly rate. A few weeks later, he wished he had accepted her flat rate when she submitted a $1,050 bill and an explanation: "Your job took a lot more time than I thought it would."

HOW LONG WILL IT TAKE TO SHOW A PROFIT?

This is a very subjective question. Each product or service needs an individual marketing plan. Some items can be sold at a profit on "direct response" space advertising or a direct mail plan. Others need the two-step approach (ads and/or sales literature produce "inquiries" and follow-up materials are sent to convert them into sales). Another approach is to sell a product on a break-even or even slight loss basis, hoping to earn nice profits by offering back-end (follow-up) items.

Although there is just no way to make any blanket assertion regarding potential profits, I would have to say that you should expect very small, if any, real profits during the first several months of your mail selling career. Like many other types of business, it does take time to establish a profitable mail order business. Over 80% of the people who launch a mail order operation throw in the towel within the first three to nine months. This is unfortunate since this business takes a lot of "git and grit" and the ability to bounce back when things look bleak (as they often will!). Also, keep in mind that many of mail order's top pros (Joe Sugarman, E. Joseph Cossman, Ben Suarez, Brainerd L. Mellinger, etc.) agree that one super success will erase several failures in mail order.

If you hit one big winner out of every five to ten attempts, you can overcome all the other setbacks and still earn substantial profits.

The mail order business is not for people who can't cope with problems. It is for those men and women who are willing to accept problems as challenges to be overcome. Only the imaginative and resourceful-type person will rise to the top of this wild and wacky, upside-down business that offers such huge potential. The plodder (a person with one basic marketing plan that works) can earn a nice living in mail order, but unlimited, million-dollar success goes to the creative doer— the person with bright ideas and the determination to put them into practice.

PROFESSIONAL ADVICE

Another major stumbling block to launching a successful mail order business is all the marginal, and just plain bad advice that is out there. No one but a pro, with several years of successful, in-the-trenches experience, should counsel others. This is not always the case. Today, many people with no hands-on experience, or worse yet, people who have only failed in their own mail order ventures, often set themselves up as counselors.

Self-publishing and mail order selling are hot topics today. In almost every major city, colleges and alternative learning centers have quickly signed up instructors to teach the thousands who hunger for this information. Far too often, the learned instructor is a dolt, who cannot provide meaningful help. Worse yet, many give reams of misleading advice.

Good advice on the topics of publishing, marketing, advertising, etc., is difficult to discover. Before you ever enroll in a class, find out all you can about the teacher. Is he or she now involved in a highly successful business? Has he/she ever been? Don't waste your time or money on seminars or courses that are being taught by the incompetent or the unknowledgeable.

The hoards of bad instructors today remind me of a mail order operator I met in Minneapolis over 15 years ago. He was a printer who tried to sell, very unsuccessfully, novelty printed items by mail. Nothing worked, and he lost several thousands of dollars his first two years in mail order. Then he got the bright idea to write a booklet on how to get rich in mail order. He gave his manuscript a snappy title and it became a good seller. At a meeting of the Twin Cities Mail Order Club, he astonished me and twenty other attendees with this comment: "It's easier to make money in mail order telling others how to do it, than by doing it yourself!"

Although I have long ago lost track of this character, it would not surprise me if today he is teaching others how to make a fortune in mail order at some college or alternative education class or seminar.

No one who hasn't been on the front lines, been successful in the battle for profits, has the moral right to send others into combat.

HOW MUCH CAPITAL DO YOU NEED?

Many of today's profitable mail order dealers and companies started with very limited capital. Even today, many ads still claim:

"Get started in mail order for less than $100,"

or

"Start your own mail selling business
without cash."

Horse feathers! Costs being what they are in the late 1980s, you need some capital to launch any kind of business, even a part-time, small, home-based mail order information business. It will be almost impossible to start, even in your spare time, without at least a few hundred dollars.

After all, stationery, stamps, ads (even small ads), etc., do cost money. It's true you can get started in mail order with a modest sum (and today a few hundred or even a few thousand is a modest amount), but you *do* need some seed money.

If you're really hurting for start-up funds, consider taking in a partner who has money to invest. If you draw up a comprehensive business plan, and can show that your ideas have an excellent chance for success, even venture capitalist money is possible.

Don't overlook a printer as a potential partner or investor. You'll be working closely with printers in this business, so they do make logical investors or part-owners of an information by mail business.

If you are willing to take all the risks yourself and are after all the rewards (a pretty good way to go!) you'll have to beg, borrow or earn the seed money to get started. Nobody said it would be easy, but you can do it. And you can make big money faster in this field than any other business I know of. Good ideas and good marketing can make you rich. I'm going to do my best to get your creative juices flowing, and I'll give you both innovative and proven marketing/advertising advice. If you possess a spoonful of common sense and a big dash of desire, you'll be on your way!

POTENTIAL PROFITS

From a great spare time income to great wealth, the sky is truly the limit in the mail order information business. You can get started with limited capital (but you *do* need *some* money!) and build your business into something special, starting from scratch.

Best of all, you'll find this exciting business to be a true joy. You'll hit the floor running every morning, and hurry home from your regular job at night. You'll know the exhilaration of building your own business and watching it steadily grow bigger and better. Before you know, you can be totally in business for yourself.

Writing, publishing, distributing and mail order bookselling have provided me with a first-class lifestyle (the nice homes, big fancy cars, dream vacations) over the years, and I'm eager to share this gold mine of knowledge with you.

I want you to read this book carefully and digest everything I will be presenting.

A "second reading," ten days or two weeks after you originally read it, is a darn good idea. I'm giving you ideas, systems, and strategies that really work. I also want to give you information on how to avoid all the mistakes I and others I personally know, have made in the past. Knowing what *not* to do is almost as important as knowing *what* to do. I'll tell you a good deal about both.

Chapter 5

HOW TO GET THE BEST JOB AT THE BEST PRICE FROM PRINTERS

If you are going to sell books (or anything else) by mail, you are going to be using the services of printers. While the teaching of in-depth typography and printing technology go beyond the scope of this book, I will give you the "nuts and bolts" of successfully dealing with the various kinds of printed matter and the printers you will most likely be using to produce your books, manuals, reports, catalogs, newsletters, circulars, business stationery, etc.

ALL PRINTERS AREN'T EQUAL

That's absolute gospel! Printers are not equal in service, quality and press room capabilities. And when it comes to price, the difference can be as dramatic as the climate in St. Petersburg, Florida in July, and St. Paul, Minnesota in January. Truly a world apart!

The first rule is: *visit (if at all possible) several printers and obtain several quotes on everything you plan to print. If you decide to do business with mail order printers (their prices are often very good), do so only with a firm that has a good reputation.*

Now let's explore the different types of printers who can best handle each individual job.

Book Printers

If you need a full-size book (100 pages or more) printed in either paperback or hardcover, your business should be placed with a company that specializes in printing full-sized books. Local instant printers will *not* be able to handle this job. However, some will gladly accept this kind of work, and then "farm it out" to someone else who has the capacity to do it, jacking up the price in the process.

Get all your quotes (at least 3 or 4) and ultimately place your order with a full-scale book printing house.

There are two methods which are used to print 8½x11 manuals, and 5½x8½ or 6x9 squarebound paperbacks (like the one you now hold in your hands), often referred to as a *trade paperback*, or clothbound or caseback hard cover books, of the same sizes.

Letterpress is an ancient method that uses a linotype machine to set "hot type" (metal type) which is set and then placed on the press. Photo-offset is the modern method (99% of today's books are photo offset printed) where original work is prepared by either a photo composition machine (typesetting) or simply from the composition of a typewriter. While either process may be used to print books by the photo-offset method, the modern typesetting machines almost always improve the appearance of the type, since many different styles and sizes can be employed.

Two of the most readable styles for books are "Goudy" and "English Times" (which you are reading now). Text size for books are usually 10 point on 11 leading, or 11 point on 12 leading (what you are seeing now), which is slightly larger and easier to read. The smaller the typesize the more words you can put on each page. However, easy readability is a strong factor that must be given consideration.

Text in this size—6 point—would look like this. Too small for easy readability.

TYPE SIZES

6 pt. ABCDEFGHIJKLMNOPQRSTUVWXYZ12345678910ABCDEFGHIJKLMNOPQRSTUVWXYZ123456

8 pt. ABCDEFGHIJKLMNOPQRSTUVWXYZ12345678910ABCDEFGHIJKLM

10 pt. ABCDEFGHIJKLMNOPQRSTUVWXYZ12345678910AB

11 pt. ABCDEFGHIJKLMNOPQRSTUVWXYZ123456789

14 pt. ABCDEFGHIJKLMNOPQRSTUVWX

18 pt. ABCDEFGHIJKLMNOPQRS

24 pt. ABCDEFGHIJKLM

30 pt. ABCDEFGHIJ

36 pt. ABCDEFG

48 pt. ABCD

60 pt. AB

72 pt. A

This is a sample of the most common typesizes available.

Here is text in 14 point. Too large, unless your audience is reading impaired.

Although books can be printed in all shapes and sizes, stick to 5½x8½, 6x9 or 8½x11, all standard sizes, if you desire the most cost-effective printing. Books can also be economically printed in large quantities in a small 4x7" paperbound size (the size of today's mass market paperback books). However, the public is used to buying these smaller books everywhere (bookshops, department stores, supermarkets, etc.) at relatively low prices, as a read-and-throwaway commodity. Information marketers cannot compete with the big publishing corporations who usually crank out a couple of hundred thousand, or more, of these small paperbacks, and we certainly do not want our information to be considered a quickly disposable item, like yesterday's newspaper.

For us, when we do wish to publish full-size books, the larger standard formats serve our purpose best.

Booklets, Reports & Directories

These smaller formats, which can be sold by mail at big markups, lend themselves to a wide range of production means. I like to see a full-size book professionally typeset, pasted up and printed. Even if mail sales are the publisher's primary market, a nice printing job will lend itself to the consideration of other potential markets (bookstores, libraries, etc.). With booklets, reports and directories, sales to retail outlets will be highly unlikely, although public, corporate and school libraries remain a possibility, depending on the contents.

Since *appearance* (so important to retail sales) is not the issue here, we can cut corners if we so choose. While a good strong title is no less important, we can print our report or booklet with or without style or illustrations. We can also have our manuscript prepared for press by simple typing rather than the more elaborate and more costly typesetting process. Still, I recommend that a nice, neat job is called for.

TYPESTYLES

6, 8, 10, 11, 14, 18, 24, 30, 36, 48, 60, 72 pt.

Bodoni Bold Cond.

Cooper Black

COPPERPLATE L
COPPERPLATE H

English Times
English Times Ital
English Times Bold
English Times Bld Ital

Franklin
Franklin Cond.
Franklin Cond. It.
Franklin XCond.

Goudy Oldstyle
Goudy Italic
Goudy Bold

Microstyle Extended
Microstyle Bold Ex

Ronda

Serif Gothic Regular
Serif Gothic Bold
Serif Gothic Heavy
Serif Gothic Outline

Souvenir Medium
Souvenir Med. Ital.
Souvenir Bold
Souvenir Bold Ital.

Tiffany Demi
Tiffany Heavy

UNCLE SAM OPEN

Univers 55
Univers 56
Univers 65
Univers 66

Original Script
Commercial Script
Park Avenue
Old English

Obviously, with the advent of the computer and desktop publishing available from Apple's MacIntosh, among others, any publisher with this equipment can turn out a professional job as quickly and cost-effectively as another publisher who pecks away at a standard typewriter.

Almost any sheet-fed photo-offset printer can print reports and booklets. Therefore, the decision of choice should be made on the basis of price, quality and service. For smaller directories, folios, booklets and reports, I urge you not to stop with just 3 quotes. Obtain no less than 5 or 6. Request samples of the printer's work and get firm quotes on pricing and time of delivery. Unlike the perfect-bound paperbacks or cloth or case (glued) bound hardbacks, the binding of information in smaller sizes can be done through spiral binding equipment, or by simply using staples. *Saddle stitching,* a process where two or more staples are placed in the spine of the report or booklet, is a common method to bind materials like small directories, booklets and reports being either 5½x 8½ or 8½x11 inches. Of the two sizes, the larger 8½x11 size often makes a report or small directory look more impressive. Although I have grouped directories here with booklets and reports, I stress I'm referring to small (in number of pages) directories. Large directories, containing 100 pages or more, would be grouped with manuals and full-size books, and probably should be printed in the same way, perfect bound in paperback or printed in a hard cover format.

HARDCOVER OR PAPERBACK?

If you intend to publish a full-size book or manual, you will have to choose between a hardcover or paperback format. It's really an individual decision, but to help you make the best decision, here are some of the pros and cons.

A hardcover edition is often considered more prestigious. Because of this fact, a hardback will usually justify a much higher price than a paperback.

On the other side of the coin, you'll pay more to print it and to mail it. Also, some book buyers think of hardbacks as being far less portable than paperbacks.

Paperbacks, in all sizes, dominate book publishing today, and are highly accepted by book buyers. They cost considerably less to print (the same book in hardback that costs $2.50 each for 5,000 copies, is likely to cost 75¢ to $1.00 less per copy, in paper), and also much less to mail. The major negatives would be some perception that a paperback is not as important as a hardcover, and the fact that they cannot handle the same degree of wear and tear as a clothbound or quality case-bound hardcover.

Personally, I used to lean heavily toward the publication of hardbacks, but I have since revised my thinking. Lower costs in all areas of production, warehousing and shipping, plus high consumer acceptance, makes paperbacks very desirable. If you intend to sell information strictly by mail order, realize a large portion of your buyers care little about the format you use. They simply want your information. A pleasing presentation, which is easy to read, is important, but overall format and design may be a greater concern to you than to the end user.

10 WAYS TO SAVE MONEY PRINTING BOOKS

(1) Get Several Quotes. Request quotes from several of the book printers in my source guide, plus any book printers in your area. Don't be afraid to deal with a printer in another city or state, as long as they are well established and have a good reputation. From San Diego, California, we deal with printers in four different states.

(2) Submit Your Job "Ready to Print". All editorial changes should be made *before* you submit your job to your book printer and/or typesetter. Most companies charge excessively when they have to make any changes before going to press.

(3) Have Your Camera-ready Copy Uniformly Prepared. In this way pre-printing camera work (plate-making) will require no extra work that would mean extra charges.

(4) Stay Away From "Bleeds." (Ink covering borders). Unless absolutely required, don't use copy that bleeds. Pre-press time always increases when bleed copy is used.

(5) Screens Give Copy a Multi-Color Look. Instructions to your printer to screen some of your copy (especially on your book's cover, can make a one-color job appear to be colors, and with the use of some screening, a two-color job can be made to look like three or four colors were used.

(6) Ask Your Printer to Help You Keep Costs Down. His or her recommendations concerning size, color and paper could help you save lots of money.

(7) Typewriter vs. Typesetting. It's okay to have a book simply typewritten, and it will save money. However, type-setting does improve appearance and looks more professional. Your choice! Also, it will generally save you half the cost of getting your book typeset if you deal direct with the type-setting company, rather than letting the printer farm it out and mark up the price, usually by 100%. Get several quotes from typesetters (look under Typesetting in the Yellow Pages). Prices can vary greatly here too.

(8) Don't Demand a "Rush Job." Plan your printing in advance, allowing plenty of extra time. Even the good print-ers and typesetters are frequently a few days behind schedule. Rush jobs often irritate printers, increase the risk of mis-takes, and can cost more.

(9) Pay Your Printing and Typesetting Bills Promptly! Good credit with printers and typesetters is good business. A history of paying your printing bills quickly may get you more desirable terms on future book publishing.

(10) Use Pre-Publication Sales to Make Money Before Your Book is Printed. Offering pre-publication discounts of 20% to 40% to previous book-buying customers is a good way to obtain some of the money needed to pay for a new book. These offerings should be mailed 60 to 75 days prior to your book delivery, with discount orders accepted up to 30 days of your anticipated date when you will have copies of the new book.

OBTAINING LETTERHEADS, FLYERS, BROCHURES, ETC.

Most business stationery, circulars, etc., can be produced by almost anyone who is a printer. Again, price, quality and service is your main criteria. Check out several shops locally and write for price sheets and samples from mail order printers in my Source Guide.

ENVELOPE PRINTING

Don't have your envelopes printed (unless you need a small quantity, and in a hurry) from your average instant printer. Prices are generally far too high. By placing your business with an envelope manufacturer who also offers imprinting, you'll save a bundle. Minimum orders accepted vary, but you will probably be expected to purchase at least 5,000, possibly even 10,000 at a time. I think this is fair for factory-to-you prices.

Envelopes are non-perishable and store easily. Just don't load up on them if you are contemplating a change of address. Ditto for almost all forms of printed matter. (See listing of envelope manufacturers in Source Guide section.)

PRINTING BROKERS CAN OFTEN SAVE YOU MONEY

The knock on printing brokers is: he or she is a "middle-man" who makes a commission for bringing printers and clients together. While that is true, it doesn't have to be negative. We've done some very good and cost-effective business with print brokers. These people often hustle for several different printing firms. They learn who is snowed under with business, and who is hurting for more business. They can often get you a good price on your printing needs. Their commission is paid by the printer. Just be certain to get samples of the printer's work, firm price and delivery quotes. Also, request references from the broker.

REQUEST FOR QUOTATION
BOOK PRINTING

To:

Please quote your best price for printing the following book from our camera-ready copy or negatives (please quote both ways and please quote within 10 days).

SPECIFICATIONS:

Name of book: *The Honest to Goodness Get Rich Quick Book*
Total no. of pages: 150
Trim size: 6" x 9"
Paper: Inside—60# white offset, book
Soft cover—12 pt. C1S cover
Ink: Text—black ink
Cover—two color with plastic coating
Packing: In tightly sealed cartons (no more than 50 books per carton)

QUOTE:

First printing of 5,000:   7,500:   10,000:
Reprinting of 5,000:   7,500:   10,000:

Delivery will be:_____ working days from receipt of artwork or negatives.

Terms to be arranged before work starts.

Remarks:_____

__._____

_____

Signed:_____ Date:_____

Please send two samples of books you have recently printed.

Example of a request for quotation of book printing

REQUEST FOR QUOTATION
Typesetting and Pasteup
(Please quote within 10 days)

To:

_____

_____

_____

Title:	*Anna Westmoreland's Health & Beauty Guide*
Total No. of Pages:	220
Trim Size:	6" x 9"
Typestyle:	English Times, 10/12

We desire camera-ready copy, not negatives.

PLEASE QUOTE:
- (A) Total typesetting charge
- (B) Total pasteup charge
- (C) Six photographs requiring halftones, 50% reduction and screening
- (D) Four line drawings requiring 33% reduction
- (E) Delivery charge (if any)
- (F) How many working days will be required (from the time we submit rough copy) till we have proof copy?

Terms to be arranged before work starts.

Remarks:_____

_____

_____

Signed:_____ Date:_____

Example of a request for a typesetting/pasteup quote

Braun-Brumfield, Inc.

A SUBSIDIARY OF HERITAGE COMMUNICATIONS INC   BOOK MANUFACTURERS

100 N. Staebler Road ● Box 1203 ● Ann Arbor, Michigan 48106 ● Phone (313) 662-3291

We're Growing to Serve You

Thank you, customers, for helping us to grow.
We've been serving book publishers for over 30 years.
We are specialists in short and medium run book
manufacturing with complete in-plant facilities.

- Composition with Interface
- Prepress
- Offset & Cover Presses
- Case, Perfect Binding
- Fulfillment/Mailing

- Reprints
- Journals
- Trade & Textbooks
- Reference Books
- Catalogs

We'd like to tell you more
about Braun-Brumfield, Inc.
Write for our brochure.

Offices and Plant
100 N. Staebler Road
P.O. Box 1203
Ann Arbor, Michigan 48106
Representatives in New York,
San Francisco, Chicago,
Washington, D.C., Ann Arbor,
Philadelphia

Publishers swear by us.

Who are they? Hard- and soft-cover book publishers,
and associations and societies that publish books,
journals, proceedings, directories, and manuals.

Why? They swear by us for two important reasons:
First, we're big enough for most publishing jobs, yet
small enough to provide the quick turn-around service
so many publishing projects require these days.
Second, because we combine a quality product with
competitive prices.

Who are we? Book-mart Press, one of the fastest-
growing, independent full-service printers in the metro-
politan area, serving the publishing industry nationwide.
Call or write to invite us to estimate your next job. You'll
find out why so many publishers swear by us, not at us.

2001 Forty Second Street, North Bergen, NJ 07047
201-864-1887/212-594-3344

Examples of book printer ads.

84

GET MORE FOR YOUR PRINTING DOLLAR

HENRY BIRTLE COMPANY 1143 E. Colorado Street Glendale, CA 91205 (818) 241-1598	LETTER SIZE 20# BOND 8½ x 11		LEGAL SIZE 20# BOND 8½ x 14		ASTRO BRIGHT 8½ x 11		CARD STOCK 110# INDEX 67# VELLUM 8½ x 11		25% RAG BOND 8½ x 11	
Quantity	1 side	2 sides	1 side	2 sides	1 side	2 sides	1 side	2 sides	1 side	2 sides
100	5.95	11.25	6.55	12.35	6.90	13.05	7.75	14.65	8.25	15.95
200	8.50	13.80	10.25	16.20	10.65	16.95	12.20	20.05	12.95	25.05
300	11.05	15.75	14.10	19.90	14.45	20.70	16.45	24.50	17.70	26.50
400	13.60	18.95	16.65	23.55	17.45	24.35	20.75	29.15	22.35	31.35
500	15.55	21.85	18.95	26.55	20.25	28.40	24.45	34.40	26.50	38.70
1000	19.05	26.20	25.80	35.70	28.75	40.20	36.50	51.20	39.45	55.30
Add'l 100	1.70	2.50	2.40	3.40	2.65	3.80	3.50	4.90	3.80	5.35
2000	33.45	46.75	47.10	65.90	52.30	73.30	68.05	95.20	73.85	103.40
3000	51.05	66.90	54.55	·76.40	75.35	106.80	99.40	143.05	108.00	151.20
4000	61.85	86.70	89.05	124.65	99.75	139.80	130.80	183.00	142.00	198.80
5000	75.95	106.25	109.85	151.00	123.30	172.65	163.00	226.60	175.80	246.25
Add'l 1000	13.95	19.65	20.75	29.10	23.40	32.85	31.05	42.40	22.80	47.40

PLEASE GIVE UNITED PARCEL SERVICE ADDRESS

Ship to:_____ Phone_____

Address _____

Quantity........ color ....size.....x...... 1 side ( ) 2 sides ( ) _____

Quantity........ color ....size.....x...... 1 side ( ) 2 sides ( ) _____

Quantity..........color ....size.....x...... 1 side ( ) 2 sides ( ) _____

COLORED PAPER ADD 10%

canary..pink..blue..green..goldenrod..buff..ivory..salmon..tan..(add 10%) _____

Colored ink ADD $8.00 for washup ......we do not do any two color work.._____

Reductions or enlargments add $3.00......................................._____

Cutting add$1.00 per cut per 1,000   card stock add$2.00 per cut per 1,000 _____

Folding $2.00 per 1,000 sheets fold ½ ( ) reg. #10 fold ( ) #10 Z fold ( ) _____

Collating $5.00 per 1,000 sheets ...._____

Screening photos $8.00 ...._____

Stapling 2 cents per staples...... 3 hole drilling $3.00 per 1,000 sheets _____

CLOSED DECEMBER 20th TO JANUARY 2nd (CHRISTMAS VACATION) Sub total _____

EAST OF THE MISSISSIPPI ADD 15%   California Residents add sales tax ...... _____

Henry Birtle Company
total _____

1143 E. Colorado St. Glendale, Ca 91205
Phone 818/241·1598

Examples of sheet-fed mail order printer's prices. Always obtain current price sheets before ordering.

Important Note: It's possible to save money on all your own printing needs, and/or make fast money selling printing to others. Making money as a printing broker is one of fifteen fabulous money-making plans, fully detailed, in Russ von Hoelscher's incredible new money book, "The Honest to Goodness Get Rich Quick Book." (See Source Guide.)

Chapter 6

HOW TO REDUCE MAILING EXPENSES

Good news! The U.S. Postal system subsidizes your postage when you ship books by mail.

The post office grants a special fourth-class book rate. You must stamp the outside of your book packages with an imprint stamp that states:

BOOKS
SPECIAL FOURTH
CLASS RATE

In addition to a special low postal rate, you need not be bothered with the requirements called for with other types of reduced postage rate. No ZIP code sorting; no need to mail 200 identical pieces of mail at one time, etc. I have also witnessed that the delivery of "book rate" packages, over many years, is quite accurate and quite timely. Packages are seldom lost if correctly addressed, and in most cases you can get your books across the country in good speed. Most often our book packages travel from the West Coast to the East Coast within 15 days or less, with even faster delivery to other states. That's pretty good delivery. Far better than other forms of the third or fourth class mailings that can easily take 3 to 5 weeks to travel to one coast from the other.

"Book Rate" shipping gives mail order book and information sellers an edge on other mail dealers and catalog houses who must pay higher rates to ship their merchandise. To qualify for book rate shipping, the "book" must be at least 8 pages, contain no advertising, and be bound. Loose pages, newsletters, etc., do not qualify for book rate mailing.

OTHER SPECIAL RATES FOR BOOKS

When you are shipping to customers outside the United States, you may wish to ship via mail sack. To qualify for shipping at the "Direct Sacks of Print" special rate, you must be sending more than 15 pounds of books and less than 66 pounds. Within this weight limit, your individual parcels will be put in one mail sack, and you will receive the lowest possible rate. If you do not have packages that total over 15 pounds, another international postal classification, "International Parcels of Printed Matter" may apply.

When shipping your books to schools and libraries in the United States, a special "Library Rate" may be used that is even cheaper than book rate.

Your local post office branch can provide you with literature that gives you updated information on all domestic and international postage rates and requirements. Anyone doing business by mail needs this information at their fingertips.

BULK RATE MAILING

When one first enters the mail order information selling business, orders will come to you in a trickle. However, once your ads and/or direct mailings are producing orders in high volume, you may wish to save big on postage by shipping certain types of orders by bulk mail. This is the absolute cheapest way to ship. To qualify you must have a combination of individual packages, all of which are the same size and weight, which totals 50 pounds or more, or 200 or more identical pieces. Also, each identical package must weigh 3.4948 ounces, or less.

Bulk mailings must be sorted by ZIP code. In so doing, you are helping the post office prepare the mail for delivery, and in return you receive the lowest possible mailing rate. The current rate is only 12.5 cents per piece. However, talk of yet another postal hike, as this is being written, makes me remind you to always pick up literature on the current rates and requirements available at your local post office.

To use the favorable bulk rate mailing rate, you must own a bulk rate permit and number. Currently, the cost is $60 per year. Once you purchase the permit, you have 3 choices in how to use it for your mailings:

(1) *Bulk rate permit imprinted indicia by your printer on your envelopes.* This is a time-saver, but you are also announcing to the world that you're mailing third class.

(2) *Cancelled bulk rate stamps* are available from your post office. Pre-canceled often makes it seem you are mailing first class. It takes time to affix them, but they look good.

(3) *Postal meter imprints* with a Pitney Bowes or other postal meter. While not as effective in disguising third class bulk mail as the canceled bulk rate stamps, they have far more impact than the flat, "lifeless" imprinted indicia.

5 MORE WAYS TO REDUCE POSTAGE COSTS

(1) *Require that your customers pay for postage.* Example: A dealer selling a manual for $20 may wish to require $2 extra for postage and handling. You may also give the buyer an

option: *Add $1 for book rate shipping, or $2.50 for first class delivery.*

(2) *Always know the "best rate" to mail anything you ship.* Having current postal requirements and rates posted in your mailing area is a must.

(3) *In your direct mail offers, enclose a return envelope that requires the customer to affix a postage stamp.* This reduces mailing costs on Business Reply Envelopes (BRE) where you must pay not only the return postage, but also a premium for each letter delivered.

(4) *Pay other mail order dealers to enclose your brochures or circulars in their direct mailings.* There are several mail order dealers who will be happy to do this at a nominal charge of 2¢ to 5¢ per piece. Caution: if you decide to do this, make very certain that (1) the company who mails for you is mailing to the type of prospect you want to reach, and (2) that this company has a good result-getting reputation. *My experience tells me that a large number of companies who offer to mail circulars for other dealers (some offer both printing and mailing) cannot be trusted.*

(5) *Always be "Weight Conscious."* Since postage and mailing costs will always take a big bite out of your business budget, plan ahead. Know the approximate weight of everything you print or purchase for resale. Paper weight is important. Without sacrificing quality, you can often use a lighter weight and save postage.

(6) *Mail bulk rate whenever possible.* While bulk rate may be used to ship orders, it more often is used to obtain orders via direct mailings. It's a *pro and con* situation. The rate is much lower than first class, but the deliverability is not as good as first class. While large packages seem to enjoy a 99% plus deliverability rate via bulk mail, smaller envelopes do not. Many mail companies worry about this deliverability factor. Structured tests by leading catalog houses, reported in *DM News,* and other trade publications, seem to indicate that between 5% and 30% of many large bulk mailings never reach their intended addresses. Certainly the reasons are

many-fold. Mailing lists often have not been cleaned recently, and are loaded with nondeliverables. Lists also can be improperly addressed. This often is the case on mail to large apartment houses which does not contain individual apartment numbers.

While the mail order dealer or catalog company, along with mailing list owners and/or brokers, must share some of the "no-delivery" responsibility, so too must the postal system. More stringent requirements and harsh penalties should be imposed on any postal worker who willfully destroys any class of deliverable mail. Mail order companies, large and small, support and pay for our postal system. Business mail represents a far greater volume than personal mail. *The post office and the mail order entrepreneur should be partners in progress, helping make our mail system ninety-nine and forty-four, one hundredths percent perfect.* It's not an impossible dream!

With all due consideration of the potentially large nondeliverable factor, it is still most often more cost-effective to mail bulk rate, as opposed to obtaining near 100% delivery via first class, at the expense of the much higher first class rate.

Chapter 7

PRICING
YOUR PRODUCTS

The price you choose for your books or other "paper and ink" products is extremely important. Unless you have sole property rights, you are at the mercy of someone else's pricing. When you have sole rights—a product *you* create and have printed, or one that you obtain the exclusive right to market, you must price it wisely.

DON'T SELL YOURSELF, OR YOUR INFORMATION, TOO CHEAPLY

If you have created or acquired a strong information product, one that appeals to a wide audience, or one that has great interest to a smaller, but reachable segment of the population, you have something of true value. Price it with maximum profits in mind. Maximum profits here, mean the best price that the largest segment of your target market will pay. That may mean a 4 to 1 price markup to the actual total production cost, or it may mean a markup of ten times, or more, manufacturing/acquisition costs. The bigger the gross markup the better, as long as you do not exceed a price that your target market deems to be fair.

Direct mail, the personal one-to-one medium, is a great way to test pricing. Recently, I tested four different prices on a real estate investment, three-ring, loose-leaf manual for Profit Ideas. A proven mailing list of 39,000 was split A-B-C-, into three 13,000 price testing segments. The entire mailing package was identical (this is vital in price testing) except for price. The three different prices were $39.95, $49.95 and $59.95.

Here are actual response results of this 3-way price testing for this real estate investment mailing:

39,000 total pieces mailed yielded 776 orders (just slightly below a 2% overall response rate), but look at the different response per each 13,000 price segment.

13,000 mailed at $39.95 price obtained 307 orders.
13,000 mailed at $49.95 price obtained 288 orders.
13,000 mailed at $59.95 price obtained 181 orders.
Total 776 orders.

All printing and mailing costs ($354 per 1,000 pieces (each piece includes sales letter, brochure, lift letter, order form and two envelopes—outside No. 10 envelope and inside No. 6¾ return—stuffed and mailed bulk rate, are identical. Also, total fulfillment costs of $10.25 each (product, shipping container and book rate postage) are exactly the same.

Here is the breakdown:

307 orders obtained from 13,000 mailed at the price of $39.95 brings in $12,264.65. From this we deduct $4,602 (printing and mailings costs at $354 per M) and 3,146.75 (fulfillment cost of $10.25 x 307 orders); $12,264.65 in orders, less 7,748.75 (print, mail and fulfillment costs). *Gross profit: $4,515.90.*

288 orders obtained from 13,000 mailed at the price of $49.95 brings in $14,385.40. From this we deduct $4,602 printing and mailing costs, plus $2,952 fulfillment costs. $14,385.40 in orders, less $7,554 (print, mail and fulfillment costs). *Gross profit: $6,831.40.*

181 orders obtained from 13,000 mailed at the price of $59.95 brings in $10,850.05. From this we deduct $4,602

96

printing and mailing costs, plus $1,855.25 in fulfillment costs. $10,850.05 in orders, less $6,457.25 (print, mail and fulfillment costs). *Gross profit: $3,392.80.*

Now, after the fact, guess which price was best? If you say $49.95, go to the head of the class. If you say anything else, this may not be the right business for you. Only by testing prices can we know.

PRICE RESISTANCE

Supermarkets, department stores, and other retail businesses are fond of 95¢ and 99¢ pricing, such as 99¢, $1.95, $1.99, $2.95, etc., because they have the preconceived notion that a price barrier is crossed each time you add another full dollar. You and I *know* $1.99 is just about equal to $2.00, and yet, psychologically, it *appears* to still be one dollar plus some change. In mail order selling, $2.00 is probably a better price than $1.99 for some little gizmo, because of two important reasons: (1) many people don't like writing very small checks for odd-cent amounts, and (2) any item priced at $10 or less will bring a certain percentage of cash orders. Anyone sending cash would have to load up an envelope with lots of change to reach a price of $1.99 (something folks simply won't do), or "overpay" by enclosing two one dollar bills (something they also often prefer not to do).

Over twenty years experience in mail selling has taught me that even dollar amounts up to ten dollars are most desirable, and the use of cents (usually .95, but sometimes .99) is best when your price goes above $10. Therefore, $10 is as good, and quite likely a better price than $9.95 for a product sold by mail (the reverse would be true for a book being sold at a retail book shop). $19.95 however, would most often be a better price than $20 for mail order, and above a $20 level, a 95 cents tag on it is almost always the best way to price. Of course there are exceptions to any rule. For example, I have found gambling information buyers often will send cash for offers up to $50 in price, and thus, even dollar amounts up to $50 can work nicely. Also, newsletter subscription buyers seem to prefer an even dollar amount, even though they almost always pay by check or credit card, than any offer that ends in cents. Still, a $49 newsletter offer will most likely outpull a $50 offer. Unlike newsletter subscribers, magazine subscription offers work very well with 95 cents or 99 cents as a tag on. *12 issues for less than than a dollar each!* (prices set at $11.95 or $11.99 will usually work better than 12 issues for $12).

All of this just goes to illustrate how important *price psychology* blends with *perceived value* in determining if your prospect will buy or not buy. As always, his or her *desire* and perception of *the benefits in owning* is always involved in any buy or not-buy decisions.

The information marketer must carefully weigh all known facts (many available only through price testing), and also acquire a perception of what is the best price to ask. Obviously, production and/or acquisition costs will affect this decision; however, these costs alone must not dictate ultimate pricing. For many mail order sellers, underpricing, not overpricing, is a major cause of failure.

I'll never forget an idealistic, but unrealistic, lady in Riverside, California who once told me, *"I printed this book for less than $3. In good conscious, I cannot price it at more than $10."* She was having none of my suggestion that she must price her work in the $15 to $20 range in order to successfully sell her book, with large display ads in select magazines. By remaining rigid, and holding to misguided principles, she continued to lose money. Soon, she threw in the towel in disgust, and dispatched thousands of unsold books, at far less than production cost, to a book remainder dealer in New York. Big markups are not obscene, they are often essential to successfully market your information product. Production costs will always be a smaller expense than promotion and marketing costs.

SUCCESSFUL COMPETITORS HELP IN MAKING PRICING DECISIONS

Your book, manual or report may be very unique, as well

it should be. Still, it's likely that other related items are currently being sold to the same market that you're after. Get on your competitors' mailing lists, start a file that includes their ads and/or mailing packages. Also place orders for their products. Knowing what they offer and at what price will help you in your pricing.

WHAT THE MARKET WILL BEAR

Your production and other costs, your own tests, and knowing what your competitors are doing, combined with all the benefits you can put in both the product and the promotion of the product, will determine your ultimate price. If that adds up to many, many times basic costs, rejoice! Mail order fortunes are made by women and men who provide their customers something of real value, at a real good price. If you hope to become wealthy selling information by mail, you must obtain as good a price as the market will bear, and respond to, in large numbers.

THE NET WORTH OF YOUR CUSTOMER

Pay close attention. This is important stuff. Very few mail order information marketers are able to stay in business and prosper with one-shot propositions. Almost always it is essential to obtain crucial repeat business and follow-up profits. You must have additional products (yours, those obtained from others, or most likely a combination of both). Although we'll discuss bounce-back and follow-up offers elsewhere in this book, determining the net worth of each customer you obtain fits well in this chapter on pricing.

The net worth of each customer you obtain is determined by the aggregate profit you can make per customer during the span of time that he or she actively responds to your offers.

Many successful mail order information sellers have found that the initial dollar amount received from a new customer represents only 10% to 20% of the total amount that person will spend during the time they remain an "active customer."

Let's use the higher 20% figure and work up some interesting mail order math:

As an example, let's say you sell a book or directory for $20 (or $19.95) as your initial business with a new cient. If, on the average, each of your customers spend 20% of the total dollar amount they will ultimately spend with you, on their first order, and do so over a one and a half year period (assuming that they become inactive after 18 months), then each new customer you obtain is ultimately worth $100 to you in gross sales. The exact net profit would be how much remains after deducting all expenses.

This is vital knowledge to have. If every one of your customers, on the average, makes purchases worth $100 (obviously, the gross and net worth of every customer could be less or greater than this amount we are using in this example), this can be another big factor in all your pricing decisions. Realizing we can realistically obtain 80% additional business from our original customer in a most cost-efficient manner (bounce-back package inserts and follow-up mailings will take a much, much smaller bite out of bottom line profits than mailings or ads needed to get original orders), we may be enticed to offer more for less to attract each valuable new customer.

As a new information entrepreneur, you may have to seek every dime the market can possibly bear with your original offer. Nevertheless, good record-keeping on the ultimate gross and net worth of each customer, determined by repeat order patterns, will give you great insights into how best to structure and price your initial offer, once you establish yourself and are not operating from a month-by-month "survival" position.

In some cases, it's even ultimately good business and profitable to be willing to lose money in order to obtain new customers. This is often true when selling high ticket items, courses and newsletter subscriptions. Howard Ruff, the well-known and highly successful financial newsletter publisher, once told me that his company spent well over $200 in advertising and marketing costs for each new subscriber who paid $145 for a new subscription. He was willing to accept a substantial loss to obtain each new subscriber, knowing a large percentage would choose in 12 months or less, to renew their subscription. Since renewals in newsletter publishing will cost only a fraction of the amount it takes to obtain new subscribers, the profit picture gets brighter each time a subscriber decides to renew. A "seasoned subscriber" (one who has been in the fold at least 3 years), is a solid gold customer. In addition to recouping any original marketing costs, you have made a nice profit from his subscription renewals. In addition, if you're like Ruff and other savvy marketers, you have probably sold your subscribers several books, reports and tapes. You may even have enticed him to pay handsomely to attend a workshop or seminar, to boot.

One of the splendid advantages of publishing a newsletter or magazine is the opportunity it gives you to continuously offer something new to each subscriber. A major disadvantage of subscription publishing is the high cost (often at a substantial original loss) of obtaining each new subscriber.

Returning to our simplified example of $100 in total business from each new customer we land, let's say for the point of this discussion, that this $100 melts down to a net profit of $33. (Remember, the net profit percentage on the original order may be quite small, or even non-existent, but the follow-up profit margin should be handsome on his second order, third order, etc. Once he buys and is satisfied with his original purchase, he will seriously consider any new offer you routinely send him.) Using this set of figures, each customer you secure has a net value of $33. If our records indicate we originally must spend $14 to first obtain each customer, who then ultimately yields us a profit of $33, we may wish to consider spending more, per original order, to bring us larger numbers of customers.

The net value of each customer, and the time period he or she remains "active" is information we can greatly use to estimate our projected profits. The wise mail order dealer will always (1) seek new customers and (2) do everything possible to *upgrade* customers with follow-up offers.

Aggressively work to keep postage costs within accepted limits. Keep updated on all postal rules and rate changes. Also, strive to learn everything you can about the ultimate value of each customer you obtain.

Section II

HOW TO GET RICH SELLING INFORMATION BY MAIL

Chapter 8

SUCCESSFUL CLASSIFIED ADVERTISING

THE 3 METHODS OF SELLING INFORMATION BY MAIL

To sell your books, plans, etc., by mail, you have three choices. And you can use any one, two or all three of them effectively.

(1) Large display (space) ads that ask for the order

(2) Small display or classified ads that usually only ask for an inquiry

(3) A direct mail package that goes after the order

Once you have good books to sell (yours, those of a reputable publisher, or a combination of both), you're ready to enter the exciting, potentially profitable, but also risky world of mail order advertising.

Will you use space advertising (classified or display) to sell direct from the ad or will you use the inquiry/follow-up (two-step) method?

...or is your offer more suited for a direct mail campaign?

...or will you use a combination of these methods?

Let's consider each various media method. The more you know about all available media, the easier it will be for you to make a decision on which advertising approach suits you and your chosen products best.

Let's start with a step-by-step analysis and proven approach for operating a profitable classified advertising mail order business.

TWO-STEP CLASSIFIED ADVERTISING

Many mail order entrepreneurs make their mail order starts via classified advertising. Many operators have found success using this approach. Mail order beginners with limited advertising knowledge and/or limited cash are often best advised to "test the mail trade waters" in this medium.

A short (20 words or less), well-written classified is often the lowest cost-effective method of advertising with the best overall dollar-for-dollar return. The key to success is first get large numbers of inquiries, and then sell a substantial percentage of that number of original responses.

As with display ads, you must be certain that your classified ads are in the correct media. Start by researching (your public library is a good place to begin) all potential media for your particular offer.

LOOK FOR THE MEDIA AND
CHECK OUT THE COMPETITION

Write to every single publication that accepts classified advertising which seems even "remotely right" for

Advertising Director
Opportunity Magazine
Chicago, IL

Your publication is being considered as an
advertising medium for our 344 page manual,
A Treasury of Home Business Opportunities.

Please forward your media package to
include an ABC statement of circulation,
your reader-ship demographics, a recent
sample copy, and an advertising rate card.

Would you like us to send you a review copy
of this new hardcover book?

Please place us on file to be notified of future
rate or policy changes. Thank you.

Sincerely,

Russ von Hoelscher

RVH:ml

Sample letter to receive sample copy and publication's
circulation, rates, etc.

National Mail Order Classifieds, (PO Box 5, Sarasota, FL 33578) is a leading agency in placing classified ads.

Word Rate Chart

NATIONAL MAIL ORDER CLASSIFIED
P.O. BOX 5 — SARASOTA, FLA. 33578

Use this handy word rate sheet to figure cost of your ads when ordering.

50¢ WORD RATE TABLE

10	$5.00	20	$10.00	30	$15.00
11	5.50	21	10.50	31	15.50
12	6.00	22	11.00	32	16.00
13	6.50	23	11.50	33	16.50
14	7.00	24	12.00	34	17.00
15	7.50	25	12.50	35	17.50
16	8.00	26	13.00	36	18.00
17	8.50	27	13.50	37	18.50
18	9.00	28	14.00	38	19.00
19	9.50	29	14.50	39	19.50

$1.50 WORD RATE TABLE

10	$15.00	20	$30.00	30	$45.00
11	16.50	21	31.50	31	46.50
12	18.00	22	33.00	32	48.00
13	19.50	23	34.50	33	49.50
14	21.00	24	36.00	34	51.00
15	22.50	25	37.50	35	52.50
16	24.00	26	39.00	36	54.00
17	25.50	27	40.50	37	55.50
18	27.00	28	42.00	38	57.00
19	28.50	29	43.50	39	58.50

$3.95 WORD RATE TABLE

10	$39.50	20	$79.00	30	$118.50
11	43.45	21	82.95	31	122.45
12	47.40	22	86.90	32	126.40
13	51.35	23	90.85	33	130.35
14	55.30	24	94.80	34	134.30
15	59.25	25	98.75	35	138.25
16	63.20	26	102.70	36	142.20
17	67.15	27	106.65	37	146.15
18	71.10	28	110.60	38	150.10
19	75.05	29	114.55	39	154.05

75¢ WORD RATE TABLE

10	$7.50	20	$15.00	30	$22.50
11	8.25	21	15.75	31	23.25
12	9.00	22	16.50	32	24.00
13	9.75	23	17.25	33	24.75
14	10.50	24	18.00	34	25.50
15	11.25	25	18.75	35	26.25
16	12.00	26	19.50	36	27.00
17	12.75	27	20.25	37	27.75
18	13.50	28	21.00	38	28.50
19	14.25	29	21.75	39	29.25

$1.95 WORD RATE TABLE

10	$19.50	20	$39.00	30	$58.50
11	21.45	21	40.95	31	60.45
12	23.40	22	42.90	32	62.40
13	25.35	23	44.85	33	64.35
14	27.30	24	46.80	34	66.30
15	29.25	25	48.75	35	68.25
16	31.20	26	50.70	36	70.20
17	33.15	27	52.65	37	72.15
18	35.10	28	54.60	38	74.10
19	37.05	29	56.55	39	76.05

$4.25 WORD RATE TABLE

10	$42.50	20	$85.00	30	$127.50
11	46.75	21	89.25	31	131.75
12	51.00	22	93.50	32	136.00
13	55.25	23	97.75	33	140.25
14	59.50	24	102.00	34	144.50
15	63.75	25	106.25	35	148.75
16	68.00	26	110.50	36	153.00
17	72.25	27	114.75	37	157.25
18	76.50	28	119.00	38	161.50
19	80.75	29	123.25	39	165.75

95¢ WORD RATE TABLE

10	$9.50	20	$19.00	30	$28.50
11	10.45	21	19.95	31	29.45
12	11.40	22	20.90	32	30.40
13	12.35	23	21.85	33	31.35
14	13.30	24	22.80	34	32.30
15	14.25	25	23.75	35	33.25
16	15.20	26	24.70	36	34.20
17	16.15	27	25.65	37	35.15
18	17.10	28	26.60	38	36.10
19	18.05	29	27.55	39	37.05

$2.50 WORD RATE TABLE

10	$25.00	20	$50.00	30	$75.00
11	27.50	21	52.50	31	77.50
12	30.00	22	55.00	32	80.00
13	32.50	23	57.50	33	82.50
14	35.00	24	60.00	34	85.00
15	37.50	25	62.50	35	87.50
16	40.00	26	65.00	36	90.00
17	42.50	27	67.50	37	92.50
18	45.00	28	70.00	38	95.00
19	47.50	29	72.50	39	97.50

$4.50 WORD RATE TABLE

10	$45.00	20	$90.00	30	$135.00
11	49.50	21	94.50	31	139.50
12	54.00	22	99.00	32	144.00
13	58.50	23	103.50	33	148.50
14	63.00	24	108.00	34	153.00
15	67.50	25	112.50	35	157.50
16	72.00	26	117.00	36	162.00
17	76.50	27	121.50	37	166.50
18	81.00	28	126.00	38	171.00
19	85.50	29	130.50	39	175.50

$1.25 WORD RATE TABLE

10	$12.50	20	$25.00	30	$37.50
11	13.75	21	26.25	31	38.75
12	15.00	22	27.50	32	40.00
13	16.25	23	28.75	33	41.25
14	17.50	24	30.00	34	42.50
15	18.75	25	31.25	35	43.75
16	20.00	26	32.50	36	45.00
17	21.25	27	33.75	37	46.25
18	22.50	28	35.00	38	47.50
19	23.75	29	36.25	39	48.75

$2.95 WORD RATE TABLE

10	$29.50	20	$59.00	30	$88.50
11	32.45	21	61.95	31	91.45
12	35.40	22	64.90	32	94.40
13	38.35	23	67.85	33	97.35
14	41.30	24	70.80	34	100.30
15	44.25	25	73.75	35	103.25
16	47.20	26	76.70	36	106.20
17	50.15	27	79.65	37	109.15
18	53.10	28	82.60	38	112.10
19	56.05	29	85.55	39	115.05

$4.95 WORD RATE TABLE

10	$49.50	20	$99.00	30	$148.50
11	54.45	21	103.95	31	153.45
12	59.40	22	108.90	32	158.40
13	64.35	23	113.85	33	163.35
14	69.30	24	118.80	34	168.30
15	74.25	25	123.75	35	173.25
16	79.20	26	128.70	36	178.20
17	84.15	27	133.65	37	183.15
18	89.10	28	138.60	38	188.10
19	94.05	29	143.55	39	193.05

National Mail Order Classified - P.O. Box 5 - Sarasota, Fla. 33578
Tel. 813-366-3003

the ad you have in mind, and the information you wish to sell by mail.

The *IMS/AYER Directory of Publications* and *Standard Rate & Data,* (both available to use, but not to check out, at public libraries) are great sources of all types of media. A more limited, low-priced manual of most popular sources of leading media, is the low-priced *The Directory of Leading Magazines & Newspapers*, available by mail for only $12 (see *Source Directory*).

WRITE FOR MEDIA KITS

On your letterhead, write to all potential publications, requesting their media kit (circulation, demographics, ad costs, etc.) and a current sample copy. You'll soon be eyeball-deep in magazines, newspapers, and trade journals. The next step is to select a small group of the most logical, based on both editorial slant and the ads for other items that are in some way related to what you wish to peddle.

SMALL SALES OR FREE INQUIRIES?

I have found that well over 95% of the successful classified advertisers use "two-step" inquiry advertising. Making classifieds pay on the "order direct basis" is not very easy. Still, some dealers *do* make this method pay, but only if they are selling a small booklet or some other item priced under $5.00.

Information sellers of "small booklets," "how-to plans," "recipes," etc., often are able to get cash with order from a small classified ad. Those of us who sell full-size books and manuals must use the two-step inquiry method.

Listed below are a few such cash-with-order ads that have been running for many months during the past year, leading me to believe they are working quite well for their operators.

105 ways to make big money
from your home. New booklet,
only $2. Name & address.

100% natural roach and water-
bug repellant. Only $2. It
works! Name & address.

College without campus. Earn your
degree the easy way, by mail. Information book only $3. Name & address.

Sweet potato pie. Mouthwatering
100-year-old recipe. Only $1.
Name & address.

The above sampling of classified ads should give you some insight into how some dealers are using a few words to ask for the order direct from the ad. Always remember, this only works on low-cost items.

Direct orders from classified ads do not work for most offers. However, low-priced offers (usually $3 or less) sometimes will click. Keep in mind...when you're selling items at only a dollar or two, or three, you need a flock of orders before you can make money on the proposition.

For most mail order book sellers, it is the "inquiry ads" that produce best overall results.

Here is a sampling of inquiry-type classified advertising:

Penny stocks that yield big profits.
Free report. Name & address.

Raise investment capital. New book
tells all. Details free. Name & address.

Sell words! Earn money as writer/pub-
lisher. No experience Free details.
Name & address.

111

Health—wealth—happiness. Now you
can have it all! Free information.
Name & address.

Money making money. Shrewd investing
and wealth-building plans. Free
information. Name & address.

Success! Love! Money! Power! You
can have it all! Free details.
Name & address.

Stay home and make money.
Hundreds of plans. Free
information. Name & address.

"Secrets of the Millionaires" revealed. Free details. Name & address.

Get rich quick! Up to $25,000
in 25 days. Free information.
Name & address.

Get rich in mail order selling
simple information. Free details.
Name & address.

You can achieve "Total Success"
using the Science of Mind. Free
information. Name & address.

You will notice...all of these inquiry ads have one
thing in common—they all use the magic word FREE!
If you use your advertising to generate inquiries, always
use this motivating four-letter word.

Some dealers, especially newcomers, offer free literature but request the reader to enclose a Self-Addressed
Stamped Envelope (SASE) or a loose stamp to cover
postage. This tactic will help you cut your postage bill.
It also will greatly reduce the number of replies you
receive. Overall, when advertising "free details," it is
more profitable to keep it simple and keep it easy to
reply. If you offer free information, let it be free!

THE 10 STEPS TO SUCCESS IN WRITING A DYNAMITE CLASSIFIED AD

(1) Learn to know your buyer as much as possible about the wants, needs, and motivation of your potential customer.

(2) *Start a "Swipe File"* (a file of ads from the competition). Pay much attention to the classified ads of successful competitors (any classified that continues to run "as is" for six months or longer, probably is working very well).

(3) *Write a long ad.* List all the benefits, real and perceived of your product. Write 60, 80, 100 words, or even more. Then begin omitting everything but the most important 15 to 25 words you have written.

(4) *Once you have a good ad, rewrite it to make it better.*

(5) *Make the headline "scream"!* Here are a few powerful examples: *Get rich quick!; Women will notice you!; A split second in eternity; The world's best tasting beer.* Now are you getting the idea? You are? Good!

(5) *Don't forget to use the word FREE.* It's still a magic word.

(6) *Keep everything short and concise.* You're paying by the word, and you do want to keep ad costs down while still delivering a powerful message.

(7) *Abbreviate your name and address.* You may be the Pathways Book Publishing Company, Suite 1000, 1825 Baltimore Dr., La Mesa, CA 92041, but that's too many words. So let's "rename" you (for the purpose of our classified): Pathways, 1825 Baltimore Dr., #1000-C, La Mesa, CA 92041. A lot less words, and thereby less cost.

(8) *Key all of your ads.* Good record-keeping is a must with 2-step classified advertising. You want to know (a) how many inquiries every ad you run pulls, and (b) what percentage of inquiries become orders. In the above address (#7), I have tacked on a key to the suite number—#1000-C, with the "C" being the key. To keep track of the actual orders, it's simple to key the order card.

(9) *Now that you have an attention-getting ad, how can you make it better?* I hope you get my drift—*rewrite till you get it right.* We don't want a good classified inquiry ad—we want a great one!

(10) *The right media is a must, and so is the right classification.* Your competition can help you make a classification decision. If you're selling moneymaking information, the *Business Opportunities* or *Financial* classifications probably work best. If you sell health information, a *Health/Beauty* should pull best, and so on. IMPORTANT: stay out of any classification labeled: *Books, Booklets,* etc. That may be what you're technically selling, but they usually do not pull inquiries anywhere near as well as more specific classifications. A person interested in a business or moneymaking venture isn't shopping for a book or booklet. He or she is looking for opportunity! Your packaging (book, report, booklet, etc.,) is not very important to this person. Hopefully your information is of great importance. Be specific in choosing your classification and results can multiply.

CLASSIFIED ADVERTISING TESTS

Once you have rate cards from dozens, or even hundreds, of potential media, you can make your *primary choices* for your initial tests. No more than 10% to 15% of your overall classified advertising budget should go into this first round of tests.

That percentage, and the amount of your ad budget, should tell you how many publications you will be able to place initial ads in. Now, to save 15% or more of your precious ad dollars, it's time to set up your own ad agency.

HOW TO ESTABLISH YOUR OWN ADVERTISING AGENCY

The next best thing to "discount advertising" (which I will discuss later) is taking an agency discount of 15% to 17% off regular rates on all advertising—classified or display—that you place.

How do you do it? Simple! Establish your own advertising agency!!

It really is quite simple to set up your own ad agency, and if you run a fair amount of ads, savings will be considerable.

Here's the easy, step-by-step procedure:

1. Use a name different than your regular mail order company name. If you're simpy using your own name to sell by mail, use some variation for your agency name. Example: John Miller Sales could start an agency as J.M. Advertising. If your company name is Mid-America Book Company, perhaps Mid-West Advertising could serve as your "agency name."

2. Register and license your ad agency name if your state requires this.

3. Have a local printer run off a couple hundred "Insertion Order" sheets (you may copy the form I have reprinted here. Type in your new agency name under "Agency").

4. Submit all of your future advertising to the media by using the "Insertion Order" form, deducting 15% from their rate cards. Most publishers also allow agencies an extra 1% or 2% for sending cash with order.

Discounts of 15% to 17% can amount to a tidy sum over a year of advertising. Money saved is money earned! Isn't it time you established your own advertising agency? Who knows, in addition to saving plenty of money on your own advertising, from time to time others may request that you place orders for them. It won't cost them a penny more, and you then could pocket up to 17% for just handling the transactions.

My own advertising agency was started just to save me money on my own space advertising, but over the years I have earned extra profits by placing ads for various copywriting clients. It is an added bonus to setting up your own ad agency to save money on your own ads.

INTERPRETATION
OF TEST RESULTS

Although mail order selling is a "numbers game," I don't believe in getting too hung up with scads of figures. While some mail dealers fill reams of notebooks with calculations of all kinds, I like the K.I.S.S. approach. By all means, compile all relevant data. You must know your average cost per inquiry for classified advertising; the percentage of inquiries that convert to orders; and how many follow-up mailings to make. In most cases of two-step classified advertising, I have discovered three follow-ups to the original mailing (a total of four mailings, each spaced approximately 2 weeks apart) works well.

But when everything is said, done, and recorded, the best interpretation of how well you're doing is the bottom line. Was it written in black ink or red? And if the ink color was crimson, will it be erased and reprinted solid black, due to business obtained from other follow-up promotions?

116

INSERTION ORDER

AGENCY: TO:

PRODUCT: DATE:

ADVERTISER:

dates of insertion	number of times	caption to read	key or code	space ordered

COPY TO READ:

SPECIAL INSTRUCTIONS & REQUESTS:

RATE:

_____times at $_____

= $_____

Check #_____

By:_____

Less____% frequency discount $_____

Less____% agency commission $_____

Less____% cash discount $_____

Net amount of this order $_____

Advertising Results

PUBLICATION _____ ISSUE_____ ON SALE_____

KEY_____ SIZE OF ADV._____ COST OF ADV. _____

PRODUCT ADV. _____

REMARKS_____

DATE	INQUIRIES		ORDERS		SALES	
	Number Received	Total to date	Number Received	Total to date	Day's Sales	Total Sales
1						
2						
3						
4						
5						
6						
7						
8						
9						
10						
11						
12						
13						
14						
15						
16						
17						
18						
19						
20						
21						
22						
23						
24						
25						

Example of ad response record sheet.

HOW OFTEN SHOULD YOU RUN
CLASSIFIED ADS IN THE SAME MEDIA?

Unlike the changes required for space (large display) ads), successful classifieds can be run with little or no changes, for many months—or even years. For testing purposes, I recommend the one insertion approach. If the media appears to be working, come back for a 3 or 4 consecutive time insertion. If it's still going nicely, send that media a "till forbid" order, which allows them to run continuously until such time as you say stop (forbid!).

Although certain months (January through April, and August through November) will out-perform the late spring through mid-summer months, or the often very slow month of December, I believe small display ads or classified ads, used to obtain inquiries, can be run year 'round. Repetition is a very positive factor.

120

Chapter 9

DISPLAY ADVERTISING

Using display advertising, often called *space advertising* in mail order trade parlance, is one of the fastest ways to make or lose money in mail order. There is a lot of big money possible in running information by mail display ads. Joe Karbo, Dean F.V. DuVall, Mark O. Haroldsen, Ben Suarez, and others have raked in many millions with space ads.

If you intend to become a modern *space millionaire,* you'll have to acquire a dual personality. On one side, you must be willing to read, research, and learn (the personality of a research librarian) all you can about profitable display advertising, beginning with this chapter. On the opposite side, you must be daring and willing to take calculated risks (the personality of a riverboat gambler).

Regardless of how well you think you know your subject matter, media and your target audience, there still is an element of "chance" in display advertising. Again, only by testing can we hope to develop a smash hit—an ad that brings in megabucks!

121

THE LARGE SPACE AD—
YOUR PASSPORT TO RICHES

Although a classified or small display ad, two-step program can be very cost-effective and profitable, more time is involved to build a big money mail order information business.

The full page 8½ x 11 ad in select magazines (which is also called a "junior page" when placed in newspapers and tabloids) can be your instant blueprint to success.

In this arena, your ad copy is everything (provided that you have placed it in the right medium—a magazine, tabloid, etc., that reaches the type of people most likely to respond to your offer). You will rise or flop with the words you present your ad readers. *Can you hit 'em over the head with your headline, and then knock their socks off with the rest of your message?*

THE 4 MAJOR ELEMENTS OF A POWERFUL, FULL-PAGE SPACE AD

(1) The headline. Numero Uno in importance. You've got to hit 'em over the head, stop 'em in their tracks, so that the reader is anxious to keep reading your message.

(2) The subhead and/or opening paragraph. (A subhead is bold copy, much smaller than the headline, but still very prominent. The opening paragraph is just that—the first paragraph of the body copy.) The headline got their attention, the subhead and opening paragraph must keep it.

(3) Benefits, benefits, and still more benefits! Your head, subhead and opening paragraph should be loaded with benefits for your potential responder. Don't save the "good stuff" for later. Your most powerful and persuasive copy comes first—not buried later in the body of your ad. If they like what they read early on in your ad, they'll probably read the whole thing. A large percentage of those who read it all will favor you with an order.

(4) A strong, money-back guarantee. This builds confidence, and tells the potential responder he or she is able to order without risk. Don't fear a strong, money-back guarantee. Even if you send your buyers a piece of "junk" *(and I sincerely hope you won't)*, only a relatively small percentage will go to the trouble of returning it. This is why several operators have scored big on a one-time basis with little booklets or short, worthless reports. Yes, some stupid dealers have made big bucks on questionable one-shot deals. Why do I call them stupid? They're stupid because they settle for a *quick score only, when they could have a quick score and a whole lot more—an ongoing, fantastic, wealth-building, golden business!!*

Don't give your information customers a bad deal. Give them a *good* deal. They'll love you for it. In both the short and long run, you'll prosper. *The law of life and success is on the side of the man or woman who has integrity and who is both a giver, as well as a receiver.*

THE HEADLINE

Pay close attention. I'm going to devote many words here on how important your ad headline is, and how you can get the best headline possible for your product.

The headline you use in your ad is of greater importance than any other factor. Often, it's more vital than all other factors combined.

THE HEADLINE MUST APPEAL TO SELF-INTEREST

A person's greatest interest is his self-interest. The Mother Teresas of the world are rare. Objective Interpersonal Psychology and the Science of Mind

123

illustrates why this is so. Our eyes are the windows of our world, and we can only relate to our world through a sense of self. Even the few saints in this world (and may God richly bless them), who help so many, ultimately do so because they believe it is for their highest good, and the good of others, that they do so.

If my above remarks appear to you to be philosophical or psychological in nature, you're right—they are! I have discovered effective advertising to be just that. *A battle for the mind of the potential responder!*

Do you really think it's anything less than that? Check your premise! Using a large space, ask-for-the-order ad, as an example, what are we trying to do? Answer: (1) We are trying to stop a page-flipper dead in his tracks with a bold statement that we hope greatly appeals to his self-interest. If we succeed, we hope to entice him with our subheads and opening paragraph to continue reading. Once the entire ad is read, we hope we have pushed enough of his or her *basic want and need buttons* (success, greed, love, pleasure, sex, survival, etc.) that he will get up off his duff and start hunting for his stamps, envelopes and checkbook. It takes powerful, compelling copy to achieve that response!

Our battle for the respondent's mind should not be interpreted in a negative light. We're not playing for the same stakes as some religious cults, the CIA or KGB. We just want his mail order. To get it, however, we use an arsenal of direct response weaponry.

Appeals to the person's self-interest almost always work best in headlines. Make your headline shout to your readers—"here is some big benefit for you!" If you have real news to tell, get the news in the headline, along with the benefit. Also, keep your headline positive. With only a few exceptions, positive headlines work best. Telling them how they will prosper works better than telling them how to prevent losses.

Both positive thinkers and negative-type people seem

to respond best to positive ads.

SIX HEADLINES THAT FLOPPED

(1) DON'T READ THIS IF YOU HAVE ALL THE MONEY YOU NEED (business book)

(2) IS YOUR HUSBAND TRUSTWORTHY? (book on male infidelity)

(3) "PLEASE DON'T ASK ME!" (course on public speaking)

(4) YOU'RE A LOSER! (horse racing report)

(5) YOU NEED MY HELP (psychic report and cassette tape offer)

(6) WHAT WILL HAPPEN WHEN YOU DISAPPEAR? (life insurance booklet)

All six of the above are curiosity headlines, most of which are also negative. Next to negativity, curiosity headlines are also very risky and usually flop.

TEN HEADLINES (AND ADS)
THAT WORKED

- THE LAZY MAN'S WAY TO RICHES

- HOW TO WAKE UP THE FINANCIAL GENIUS INSIDE OF YOU

- $4,000 IN 24 HOURS

- SECRETS OF THE MILLIONAIRES

- START MAKING MONEY IN A BUSINESS OF YOUR OWN—AT HOME OR AWAY

- $25,000,000,000 THE GOVERNMENT HOLDS FOR YOU

- I TOOK THE PICTURE AND WAS SET FOR LIFE

- $500 A DAY WRITERS UTOPIA

- HOW TO GET RICH IN MAIL ORDER

- FREE $10 BOOK!

You will note that these 10 headlines, all for business, mail order or money making books and manuals, all have one thing in common. They're loaded with self-interest benefits. Also, they are all very positive in their presentation.

HOW TO WRITE A POWERFUL HEADLINE

I'm going to give you instructions on writing a powerful headline, even though you may be wise to hire an expert copywriter to prepare your full page and large display ads. If you're determined to take a total "I'll do it all myself" approach, you will want to do it as well as you can. Your headline is so very crucial to your ad's success or failure.

Write hundreds of possible headlines for every advertisement you are considering. Next, eliminate them one by one until the best one (in your judgment) remains.

LONG COPY WORKS AND SO CAN LONG HEADLINES

It's been proven over and over: In most cases, long, wordy ads, or long copy direct mail pieces, outpull their shorter worded brethren. The advantages of a few

The Lazy Man's Way to Riches

'Most People Are Too Busy Earning a Living to Make Any Money'

I used to work hard. The 18-hour days. The 7-day weeks.

But I didn't start making big money until I did less—a lot less.

For example, this ad took about 2 hours to write. With a little luck, it should earn me 50, maybe a hundred thousand dollars.

What's more, I'm going to ask you to send me 10 dollars for something that'll cost me no more than 50 cents. And I'll try to make it so irresistible that you'd be a darned fool not to do it.

After all, why should you care if I make $9.50 profit if I can show you how to make a lot more?

What if I'm so sure that you *will* make money my Lazy Man's Way that I'll make you a most unusual guarantee?

And here it is: I won't even cash your check or money order for 31 days *after* I've sent you my material.

That'll give you plenty of time to get it, look it over, try it out.

If you don't agree that it's worth at least a hundred times what you invested, send it back. Your uncashed check or money order will be put in the return mail.

The only reason I won't send it to you and bill you or send it C.O.D. is because both these methods involve more time and money.

And I'm already going to give you the biggest bargain of your life.

Because I'm going to tell you what it took me 11 years to perfect: How to make money the Lazy Man's Way.

O.K.—now I have to brag a little. I don't mind it. And it's necessary—to prove that sending me the 10 dollars . . . which I'll keep "in escrow" until you're satisfied . . . is the smartest thing you ever did.

I live in a home that's worth $250,000. I know it is, because I turned down an offer for that much. My mortgage is less than half that, and the only reason I haven't paid it off is because my Tax Accountant says I'd be an idiot.

My "office," about a mile and a half from my home, is right on the beach. My view is so breathtaking that most people comment that they don't see how I get any work done. But I do enough. About 6 hours a day, 8 or 9 months a year.

The rest of the time we spend at our mountain "cabin." I paid $30,000 for it—cash.

I have 2 boats and a Cadillac. All paid for.

We have stocks, bonds, investments, cash in the bank. But the most important thing I have is priceless: time with my family.

And I'll show you just how I did it—the Lazy Man's Way—a secret that I've shared with just a few friends 'til now.

It doesn't require "education." I'm a high school graduate.

It doesn't require "capital." When I started out, I was so deep in debt that a lawyer friend advised bankruptcy as the only way out. He was wrong. We paid off our debts and, outside of the mortgage, don't owe a cent to any man.

It doesn't require "luck." I've had more than my share, but I'm not promising you that you'll make as much money as I have. And you may do better; I personally know one man who used these principles, worked hard, and made 11 million dollars in 8 years. But money isn't everything.

It doesn't require "talent." Just enough brains to know what to look for. And I'll tell you that.

It doesn't require "youth." One woman I worked with is over 70. She's travelled the world over, making all the money she needs, doing only what I taught her.

It doesn't require "experience." A widow in Chicago has been averaging $25,000 a year for the past 5 years, using my methods.

What does it require? Belief. Enough to take a chance. Enough to absorb what I'll send you. Enough to put the principles into action. If you do just that—nothing more, nothing less—the results will be hard to believe. Remember—I guarantee it.

You don't have to give up your job. But you may soon be making so much money that you'll be able to. Once again—I guarantee it.

The wisest man I ever knew told me something I never forgot: "Most people are too busy earning a living to make any money."

Don't take as long as I did to find out he was right.

Here are some comments from other people. I have that, like you, they didn't believe me either. Guess they figured that, since I wasn't going to deposit their check for 31 days, they had nothing to lose.

They were right. *And here's what they gained:*

$260,000 in eleven months
"Two years ago, I mailed you ten dollars in sheer desperation for a better life . . . One year ago, just out of the blue sky, a man called and offered me a partnership . . . I grossed over $260,000 cash business in eleven months. You are a God sent miracle to me."
B. F., Pascagoula, Miss.

Made $16,901.92 first time out
"The third day I applied myself totally to what you had shown me. I made $16,901.92. That's great results for my first time out."
J. J. M., Watertown, N.Y.

'I'm a half-millionaire'
"Thanks to your method, I'm a half-millionaire . . . would you believe last year at this time I was a slave working for peanuts?"
G. C., Toronto, Canada

$7,000 in five days
"Last Monday I used what I learned on page 83 to make $7,000. It took me all week to do it, but that's not bad for five day's work."
M. D., Topeka, Kansas

Can't believe success
"I can't believe how successful I have become . . . Three months ago, I was a telephone order taker for a fastener company in Chicago, Illinois. I was driving a beat-up 1959 Rambler and had about

"*. . . I didn't have a job and I was worse than broke. I owed more than $50,000 and my only assets were my wife and 8 children. We were renting an old house in a decaying neighborhood, driving a 5-year old car that was falling apart, and had maybe a couple of hundred dollars in the bank.*

Within one month, after using the principles of the Lazy Man's Way to Riches, things started to change — to put it mildly.
● *We worked out a plan we could afford to pay off our debts — and stopped our creditors from hounding us.*
● *We were driving a brand-new Thunderbird that a car dealer had given to us!*
● *Our bank account had multiplied tenfold!*
● *All within the first 30 days!*
And today . . .
● *I live in a home that's worth over $250,000.*
● *I own my "office". It's about a mile and a half from my home and is right on the beach.*
● *I own a lakefront "cabin" in Washington. (That's where we spend the whole summer — loafing, fishing, swimming and sailing.)*
● *I own two oceanfront condominiums. One is on a sunny beach in Mexico and one is snuggled right on the best beach of the best island in Hawaii.*
● *I have two boats and a Cadillac. All paid for.*
● *I have a net worth of over a Million Dollars. But I still don't have a job . . ."*

$600 in my savings account. Today, I am the outside salesman for the same fastener company. I'm driving a company car . . . I am sitting in my own office and have about $3,000 in my savings account."
G. M., Des Plaines, Ill.

I know you're skeptical. After all, what I'm saying is probably contrary to what you've heard from your friends, your family, your teachers and maybe everyone else you know. I can only ask you one question.

How many of them are millionaires?

So it's up to you:

A month from today, you can be nothing more than 30 days older — or you can be on your way to getting rich. You decide.

Joe Karbo
17105 South Pacific, Dept. MM·
Sunset Beach, California 90742

Joe, you may be full of beans, but what have I got to lose? Send me the Lazy Man's Way to Riches. But don't deposit my check or money order for 31 days after it's in the mail.

If I return your material — for any reason — within that time, return my uncashed check or money order to me. On that basis, here's my ten dollars.

Name _____

Address _____

City _____

State _____ Zip _____
© 1978 Joe Karbo

Joe Karbo's highly successful full-page ad

How To Wake Up The Financial Genius Inside You.

"I Have Helped More Than 250,000 People Discover Exactly How To Achieve Financial Freedom."

THE DIFFERENCE

If hours, efforts, or brains are not what separate the rich from the average guy who is swamped with debts and very little income then what is?

I learned the answer to that question from an old fellow in Denver. This fellow worked in a drug store stocking the shelves. Very few people knew that he had $200,000 in the bank, all of which he had earned starting from nothing.

Within a year after meeting him, I was told and shown the same thing by a young man who had recently earned over a million dollars. By this time, I began to realize that what I was being shown was truly a remarkable and workable way to grow rich.

THE BEGINNING

I began to apply the principles and methods I had been shown. The results were amazing. I couldn't believe how easy it was, in fact it seemed too easy.

But then I met an elderly lady (83 years old) who, although not very smart, has made $117,000 using the same formula.

I then figured my beginning wasn't luck. For three and one half years, I worked hard to refine and improve on the formula that I had been shown, so that it would be easy to get quicker results.

As I did this, my assets multiplied very rapidly (160% per year) to the point that I didn't have to work any longer.

MORE LEISURE

I guess I am bragging now, but I did start spending a lot of time in our back yard pool, traveling around the country, and doing a lot of loafing.

Then one day a friend asked me how he could do what I had done.

So I began to outline the formula that I had improved to show him really how simple it was, and how he could do the same thing.

By the next time he approached me, I had written almost a complete volume on the

Mark O. Haroldsen became a millionaire in four years because he found a way to harness inflation to his benefit. Now it's your turn! *"I've found"* says Haroldsen, *"that most people just need a specific road map to follow...they can do what I've done."*

he had $5,000 cash in his pocket to boot.

I also showed him how to buy a $26,000 property for $75 down.

ANYONE CAN

You can do exactly what I did, or my close friends have done, in fact, you may well do it better. (I began doing this in my spare time only.)

It doesn't matter where you live or the size of your town or city, my formula will show you exactly how to:

● Buy income properties for as little as $100 down.
● Begin without any cash.

where and as often as you would like.

IT'S GUARANTEED

Now if you were a personal friend of mine, I know you would believe me and not need any kind of guarantee, but since you don't know me personally, I will guarantee that you will be completely satisfied and that my formula will work for you if you apply it. I will back up that guarantee by not cashing your check for 30 days, and if you for any reason change your mind, let me know and I will send your uncashed check back.

You may ask, why am I willing to share my formula for wealth? Well, simply because those of you who order my material will be helping to increase my net worth.

You shouldn't care if I profit as long as you profit. I guarantee that you'll be satisfied that my methods will help you or I'll send your money back!

"FINANCIAL FREEDOM"

To order, simply take any size paper, write the words "Financial Freedom", and send your name and address, along with a check for $10.00 to Mark O. Haroldsen, Inc., Dept. MM 2612 So. 1030 West, Salt Lake City, Utah 84119.

If you send for my materials now, I will also send you documents that will show you precisely how you can borrow from $20,000 to $200,000 at 2% above the prime rate using just your signature as collateral.

By the way, if you feel a little uneasy about sending me a check or money order for $10.00. simply postdate it by 30 days which will completely eliminate your risk.

'M3 : Mark O Haroldsen, Inc 1978

One of many unsolicited comments on my material:

".. when it came I read it. Then I read it again, and have read it about once a week since it came. No magic. No secrets. A plain, easy-to-understand, 1-2-3 way for anybody with a little patience and common sense to become totally independent within a reasonable length of time. The one book I've been looking for for at least fifteen years ..."

—*Jerry Donaho, Valdez, Alaska*

easy way for him to copy my results.

EASY TO READ

I wrote this in simple, straight-forward language so anyone could understand it.

This time my friend's questions were very specific. (He had already begun buying properties with the formulas I had been giving him.) Now he had a property he wanted to buy, but was out of cash. How could he buy it?

I not only showed him how to buy without cash, but by the time the deal was complete,

● Put $10,000 cash in your pocket each time you buy (without selling property.)
● Double your assets every year.
● Legally avoid paying federal or state income taxes.
● Buy bargains at ½ their market value.
● Allow you to travel one week out of every month.

When you send me a check or money order for $10. I will send you all my formulas and methods, and you are free to use them any-

Inquire at your local bookstore for Mark Haroldsen's "How to Wake Up the Financial Genius Inside You."

Haroldsen's famous ad

128

$4,000 in 24 Hours
Now you really can have money quickly!

Ad for my *Honest to Goodness Get Rich Quick Book*

Ad for millionaire George Sterne's *Secrets of the Millionaires* book

Combination *Secrets of the Millionaires* cassette tapes and book ad

131

Ad for two of our popular business books.

$25,000,000,000
The Government Holds For You

David Bendah's extremely successful ad

133

I took the picture & was set for life.

Ad for fast-selling book on making money with a camera

134

Result-getting ad for Jerry Buchanan's *Towers Club* newsletter

Super ad for Melvin Powers' _How to Get Rich in Mail Order_ book

My very successful ad which has appeared on *tens* ⟨
millions of media pages. Used as a 2-step approach f⟨
"Fast Start" book dealers program.

137

words in a headline is that you can blow them up into impressive, large, attention-grabbing type. However, a long benefit-laden head can work wonders, too, if it's loaded with benefits.

There are 3 ways to effectively present a long headline:
(1) Print the entire headline, regardless of length, with the same size type. Use up to 20% of the space allotted for your entire ad, for your headline.

(2) Emphasize one, two, or more words in your long headline by printing them in larger and/or bolder type.

(3) Break down the long copy into two parts—a major headline and a smaller, but still very prominent, subhead.

AIDA FOR RESULTS!

Good print advertising is simply good salesmanship in a printed format. That's why the tried and true A.I.D.A. formula continues to work so well.

A — ATTENTION
I — INTEREST
D — DESIRE
A — ACTION

AFTER YOUR HEADLINE, KEEP THEIR INTEREST WITH YOUR SUBHEAD AND OPENING PARAGRAPH

Once the headline has grabbed their interest, we have a chance at getting the order. This opportunity can easily slip away, like a big fish only lightly hooked. It's the job of our subheadline (if one is used) and/or opening paragraph (and your first sentence is especially critical) to hold interest and lead the prospect to the order form, or order instructions.

Here are proven ways to accomplish our goal, using subheads and first paragraphs:

(1) Get personal. You and I copy, with emphasis on "you", works well.

(2) Make a big user-beneficial promise. Make a grand promise (and one that you can keep!) that your potential customer should easily relate to.

(3) Reinforce the headline. If you have made a sensational claim in your headline, you may have stopped Mr. or Mrs. Reader in their tracks. However, they may be quite skeptical. Reinforcement and more positive explanation may be required.

(4) Name and explain the best aspect of your offer. This may be uniqueness, quality, low price, or any truly outstanding feature.

(5) Reduce anxiety. This is most often best accomplished by stating your strong guarantee.

While the headline is undebatably first in importance to an ad, the subhead and/or opening paragraph is also extremely helpful in gently pushing the reader on down to the *body copy* and ordering instructions.

BODY COPY

When the all-important headline has done its job, and the opening paragraph has continued to whet the appetite, the body copy needs a constant, easy to follow, flow and lots of benefits to keep the prospect headed in the right direction (to the order form).

HERE ARE 8 FACTORS OF A SUCCESSFUL AD

(1) Body copy loaded with benefits—big benefits and little benefits

(2) A strong, money-back guarantee

(3) Everything flows and reads easily. Absolutely no misunderstandings wanted!

(4) Lots of "you's" and only a few "I's" throughout the copy

(5) More short words and short sentences than long ones. Also no "holier than thou" posturing

(6) A "free bonus" if at all possible, because folks like to get a little extra for their money

(7) Easy to order instructions. Confuse 'em and you'll lose 'em

(8) Some of the benefits and all of your guarantee should be restated in the order form. Take the stress out of ordering and you'll get more orders!

WHY DOES *LONG COPY* USUALLY OUTPULL *SHORT COPY?*

The name of the direct response advertising game is benefits, benefits and more benefits! Wordy ads or multiple-page sales letters and brochures give you the opportunity to stuff more benefits in your written presentation. But will people take five minutes, ten minutes, or more to read it?

You bet they will—if you have stopped them with your headline and enticed them with your opening sentence and first paragraph.

Even a reader who only *skims* your ad is more likely to be captured by certain *pet benefits* that push his or her buttons, when the entire ad, letter, circular, or brochure is loaded with scads of benefits.

BRING ON THE BENEFITS!

At least 90% of all ads, brochures, and sales letters that I review are very heavy on self-glorification (the person, the book, the seminar, the service or the product) and very light on benefits to the potential reader, attendee or user. That's dumb. It's also ineffective. While some mention of yourself, your company, and how great your product is, may be appropriate (especially if it is done in the right way—to instill trust and confidence), the vast majority of all copy should be benefit copy. Who cares how famous, important, rich or smart you are? What potential responders really care about is how happy, popular, important, wealthy, healthy, better-looking or brilliant they can become by using what you have to offer. They want and crave benefits. Forget you—the important question is: *what's in it for me?*

You must realize that people are bombarded with all kinds of advertising, and their tendency is to hold on to their money. People aren't anxious to buy, but they *are* eager to obtain benefits. Asking them to send you their hard-earned money, by mail, is a B-I-G request. They won't do it unless they absolutely *crave* what you sell. To instill the craving that tells them "I must have this," your copy better be overflowing with benefits.

10 STEPS TO BETTER RESPONSE

Here are ten great ways to make your ads and mailings more beneficial, and thereby more responsive.

(1) State a primary benefit in your headline (ads, brochures) or your opening paragraph in letters. Capture your reader's attention quickly by telling him or her something very good that he or she can easily obtain from you.

(2) Make it believable. This is the age of great skepticism. Trust is not readily available, and to

141

overcome this fact, you must explain why so much good is possible to those who respond. How do you do this? Stress benefits! Big benefits first, but then lots of little benefits. Always remember, a small benefit (to you) could be a big benefit to your reader.

(3) Be specific. Spell out exactly what benefits are being offered. It's always more productive to state "you can make $50,000 a year with this home-based business," than to merely say, "you can make big money at home with this business opportunity." "Look and feel ten years younger in ninety days" is much stronger than saying "you'll look and feel younger in a short period of time." Be exact. Use time, dates, amounts, etc.

(4) You must understand what people really want. Example: You are offering a short course on learning to play the guitar. Your target market is young males who like music. Learning to play the guitar for self-gratification is just one very obvious benefit your potential customer wants. Other benefits most likely include: Popularity (his friends will appreciate him more); Sex Appeal (young ladies often get turned on by music and to those who can play it); and Self-esteem (expertly playing a musical instrument probably will give him have a much higher image of himself). As you can see, it's very likely that much more than mastering a musical skill is involved in deciding if he should send for this course. By considering all potential buyer motivations, you can push the right buttons, regardless of what you are offering.

(5) Include testimonials. Your claims are just that —they're your claims. Testimonials add substance. What others say about your book, product or service is often more convincing than what you say. Use as many testimonials as you can obtain, and when authorized to do so, use complete names. Full names instill more buyer confidence than the use of only initials.

(6) Use only artwork and photos that show benefits. Graphic art and/or photographs can be a big plus in

your sales literature, but only if they complement your copy. Use them to demonstrate benefits. Obviously, if you're a public speaker, a professional photo of yourself is important. But even then, don't load up your brochure with self-photos at the expense of benefit copy. Anyone who fills up space with several photos of himself has both an ego problem and printed salesmanship that has been weakened.

(7) Think and write you, not I. Good copy is always "you" copy. And copy that does not contain at least twice as many "you's" as "I's" is not stressing enough benefits.

(8) Always include a personalized letter. Your beautiful brochure may turn you on, and you may consider it the highlight of your mailing package. Nevertheless, for best results always include a "personalized' (even if mass produced) letter with each package you mail. A letter almost always increases your response. It allows you to talk benefits, one on one.

(10) Add a "Bonus Benefit" for a prompt response. People love to get a little extra for their money. If at all possible, offer a free bonus. This almost always increases results. Your freebie need not be an expensive item, but it should be something likely to appeal to the tastes or lifestyles of your readers.

THE BEST MONTHS TO RUN DISPLAY ADS FOR BOOKS

While mail order gift catalog houses often list the last quarter of the year (October through December) as their best mail order season, I have found that this is not true for mail order book and information sellers. Over twenty years of promoting my own books and other "paper and ink products," as well as helping many others promote theirs, has given me the following seasonal mail sales information.

In addition to giving you the most desirable months (January and February are the very best!), I have assigned a percentage value.

(1)	January	100%
(2)	February	96%
(3)	September	91%
(4)	October	87%
(5)	March	82%
(6)	August	80%
(7)	November	75%
(8)	July	73%
(9)	April	70%
(10)	May	64%
(11)	June	60%
(12)	December	59%

My records indicate the same ad (it's important that we compare an apple to an apple) in January or February will pull 40% more orders than the ad would receive if run in June or December. That could easily be the difference between success and failure! While I believe in remaining active year 'round, I also increase my advertising and mailing in the fall and winter, August through March, with the exception of December.

Although good display advertising months and productive direct mailing months are usually quite identical, there is one notable exception. Several book, cassette tape, and other information-type mailings made right after the fourth of July, often get a good response. On the other side, July is not always a responsive month for display ads in publications.

Your own information offer and your own tests for same may vary slightly from my listing of most favorable (January) to least desirable (December) months, but overall, I think you'll discover my charts are quite accurate.

DON'T BE MISLED
BY COVER DATES

Since many publications, especially consumer magazines, are cover-dated one or two months ahead of actual distribution dates, you must become aware of this and place your ads accordingly.

Example: December is most often a poor month to run large display ads. However, a publication with a December cover date may actually be mailed to subscribers, and distributed to newsstands, by mid-October.

If this is the case (the media kit sent by the publication will give you both cover dates and "on sale" dates), it may be worthwhile to place your ad. Pay only a little attention to a cover date, and a great deal of attention to the actual date of distribution.

BE SPECIFIC AND BELIEVABLE

Years ago you could write a successful ad built around a headline that simply stated, "New book shows you how to make big money!"

Those days are gone. Today's potential responder wants specifics, and is more than a little skeptical.

It takes a powerful, often *outrageous* headline to grab his or her attention, but a specific benefit stated in that headline is most desirable. The body copy, too, should contain many, many specific benefits, all sounding almost, but not quite, too good to be true. You can stretch their imaginations and dare them to be better, richer, healthier, or happier. Just don't stretch credibility to the point where it breaks. Your benefit must be specifically very, very good but also believable. As soon as a reader is convinced you are lying, you have lost him.

ADVERTISING WORDS THAT COMMAND ATTENTION

Here is a dynamic group of words that will get attention when used in your advertising copy.

- $_____ (specific dollar amt.)
- Amazing
- Announcing
- At Last
- Available
- Bargain
- Be (Popular, Successful, etc.)
- Beautiful
- Best
- Better
- Closeout
- Dynamic
- Easy
- Fabulous
- Fantastic
- Free
- Freedom
- Get
- Guaranteed
- Here's
- How (How to ...)
- Incredible
- Independence
- Important
- Improve
- Loving
- Magic
- Make Money
- New
- Now
- Only
- Opportunity
- Positive
- Powerful
- Profit
- Proof
- Quick
- Receive
- Revealing
- Save
- Secret
- Special
- Start
- Sex-appeal
- Startling
- Super
- Ultimate
- Unique
- Wanted
- You
- Vital

Most mail order responders have been burnt in the past. They have responded to mailings or ads that promised so much, and delivered so little. To make them respond one more time to your offer, you must make your presentation both great, and believable!

One of the most successful ads in recent years sold over one million telephones by mail at a very low price for each. While 98% of the copy told of the great bargain these phones were, the copywriter also used a little bit of ink to masterfully present the "downside" of his offer. In the ad he stated, *Everything about this special offer—quality, price and service—is better than good, except for the color choices. Phones are available in just three colors: beige, black or brown.* Since it's a fact that most people have at least one phone in one of those 3 colors, his "down side" remark wasn't really all that harmful to his ad copy. It did, however, make it appear that he was being objective and was presenting his readers with "all" the facts—an excellent approach to advertising!

In selling information by mail, we, too, must make it sound so great that the person cannot wait to receive it. But never so great that he does not believe our ad, or trust us.

A great headline and a one-to-one friendly but persuasive salesmanship approach, using copy laden with user benefits, is the secret of successful ads.

Chapter 10

MAKING MONEY WITH DIRECT MAIL

Direct mail is big business. It's well over a 100-billion-dollar industry, and it's growing bigger each year.

While most mail order beginners usually plunge into space advertising (classifieds or display) when they start a mail order venture, the majority of established mail order pros use direct mail for a large part of their business-building activities.

MAILING LISTS—THE KEY TO SUCCESSFUL DIRECT MAIL SALES

At the center of any direct mail effort is the mailing list you use. Powerful copywriting, expert printing, good graphics, etc., are very important, but mailing lists are the heart of any direct mail effort.

Mailing lists fall under three categories:

(1) In-house lists

(2) Mail response lists

(3) Compiled lists

A dealer's own in-house list is by far the firm's most precious commodity. These are the people who have ordered or inquired at least once. Within the in-house list, at the very core, are the company's "family jewels"—the multiple buyers—the best of all the house names.

The mail response lists are names who have responded to another company's offer. There are several thousands of such lists, in all fields and classifications, available on the mailing list rental market. Standard Rate & Data Services, Inc., 3004 Glenview Rd., Wilmette, IL 60091, publishes the "mailing list bibles" for both business lists and consumer lists in the "Direct Mail Lists, Rates and Data Directories." In thumbing through their huge directories, you will find many thousands of both response and compiled lists in almost any classification you could possibly think of, as well as many that probably never entered your mind.

Compiled lists are generally not as "responsive" as lists generated from actual orders and inquiries. However, in special cases, results can be satisfying when using a recently compiled list. Then too, compiled lists are often the only available means to reach a specific market. Compiled lists can be as broad as listings of millions of home owners to as selective a list as names and addresses of people who own homes valued at one million dollars or more. Thousands of compiled lists are available, and new classifications are constantly appearing. In most cases, mail order information sellers must use proven response lists to obtain good results.

One big factor concerning all types of mailing lists (yours, theirs or compiled) is recency. You should mail to your own house list at least four times or more per year. When possible, mail to rented response lists that are new on the list market or a proven list which has just recently been cleaned (with wrong addresses, no longer responsive customers, etc., removed).

"HOT LINE" MAILING LISTS WILL WORK BEST

The "hot line" list is a company's most recent buyer's name. In most cases that means buyers within the most recent 90-day period. Obviously, these names will be the most responsive.

If a company has a recent 10,000 "hotline" and a "main list" of 100,000, we should test the hotline first. If it doesn't work for us, the bigger main list most certainly won't either.

On the other hand, if the hotline pulls well for us, we must consider that there will be a drop-off in response once we begin using names from the master file.

Example: let's say we mail to the 10,000 hotline and obtain a 2% response (2 orders for every 100 direct mail pieces we mail). Rather than a gung-ho mailing to the entire big main list of 100,000 older names (all of which will be many months to many years old, although hopefully recently cleaned and updated), we would do well to test only 5,000 or 10,000 names from that company's main mailing list, realizing that response probably won't be as favorable as from its recent hotline names.

Over the years I have noted the drop off in response percentage between hot line and older names averages between 20% and 30%. Thus a 2% return from hotline names will probably fall to around 1.5% once we begin using the company's larger, and older, mail list. That's a big difference! A 25% drop in response percentage could turn a profitable direct mail campaign into a losing one. Only through tests will we know.

CHEAP LISTS— BIG MONEY WASTED

The going rate for mailing lists most likely to be rented by information sellers (opportunity seekers, book buyers, etc.) is currently (1987) $50-$75 per 1,000 names. Beware of lists costing less! Everyone likes a bargain, but I could fill many pages in this book with horror stories of mail dealers who have used "cheap lists."

Not all cheap lists are worthless, but the vast majority of them are. A company or mailing list broker who is peddling names at a big discount is often offering old response names, questionably compiled names, and/or over-used names. 99 times out of 100 that spells disaster!

The names you use will always be just a small part of the total cost of your mailing. Postage and printed matter costs will always take the biggest bite out of any direct mail budget.

You don't save money by using a cheap mailing list, you *lose* money!

Since there are many highly suspect mailing lists out there, plus more than a little "flim-flam" in the list business, it is generally a good idea to do all your mailing list business through reputable brokers, and not with someone who runs a little ad in a magazine, offering great prices on mailing lists.

Direct mail is a one-to-one medium that lets you reach a select target market. To be successful, you must use a good list.

THERE'S GOLD IN THEM NAMES!

Your own mailing list can be a chief source of additional revenue. The main purpose of your in-house list—customers or inquiries—is to generate follow-up business. A profitable secondary use of these lists is income obtained from renting your names to other mail order dealers. Profits from renting your names to other companies can be very substantial. A list renting for $60 per thousand will yield $48 to you, after paying the normal 20% brokerage fee. With some mail order operations, capital received from renting their own customer lists represents a major part of overall profits.

Trading your customer list with another mail order book company can also be an excellent way to achieve more direct mail business. In trading with a competitor, be certain you are trading like-for-like. If you are furnishing 5,000 recent buyers, you want 5,000 of their recent buyers in exchange, not a list of two-year-old buyers or a list of inquiries only.

Any dealer who doesn't want to handle his own mailing list rentals or trades, can hire a mailing list manager to handle these transactions. This can work very well in the hands of an experienced professional.

Most list managers take a 10% to 15% commission for their service. With both their managing fee and the regular brokerage commission, you (as the list owner) will receive 65% to 70% of all dollars obtained from your in-house list. That's less than the 80% you receive when you manage your own names. However, a mailing list manager with plenty of trade contacts, may easily earn his or her fee in obtaining a windfall of profitable business for you.

ARE YOU
RENTING OR SELLING?

Most mailing list transactions are rentals, not sales, and usually for only a one-time use. To avoid confusion, or the unpaid multiple use of any names you offer to the trade, make certain you and/or your list broker or manager spells this out under your terms and conditions to all users. A few "seeds" (names put on your list by you) can also help assure that no one is renting your names and using them in any unauthorized fashion.

WHAT YOU NEED TO KNOW ABOUT DATA PROCESSING

Data processing is an important element in the mail order business. Even if you barely understand the term, you soon must learn much about it.

While a personal computer could be a big help to you, many successful mail order operators "farm out" their data processing needs. This is your choice to make: in-house or an outside service. Several dealers use a combination of both.

In your dealings with computers, you should always remember that they are not *magical electronic brains.* You'll never get better information out of them than what you put into them. They can be helpful servants, but most definitely are not all-knowing.

You can use the data processing powers of the computer in any of several ways:

(A) Individual order processing

(B) Current order retention

(C) Current customer or hotline maintenance

(D) Master list maintenance

(E) Best customer (multiple buyer) maintenance

HOW YOU'LL RECEIVE YOUR ORDERS

A typical information by mail business will receive orders (either from ads or mailings) in the form of a coupon or order card. The order coupon will give us information on 7 important elements.

(1) What is being ordered

(2) The price of what is being ordered

(3) The "key code" (source media of order)

Mail to: **PROFIT IDEAS,** Dept. A15
8361 Vickers, Suite 304,
San Diego, CA 92111

YES! I want to make money at home.

Rush me a copy of *A TREASURY OF HOME BUSINESS OPPORTUNITIES* by Russ von Hoelscher. Enclosed is $14.95 plus $1.00 for postage/handling (Calif. residents must add 6% sales tax). I understand my satisfaction is 100% guaranteed or I may return the book within 90 days for a full refund.

I'm paying by ☐ Check   ☐ Money order

☐ Mastercard   ☐ VISA   Total: $_____

If using credit card, acct.#_____

Exp. Date_____Signature_____

Name_____

Address_____

City, State, Zip_____

Example of order coupon containing all **7** ordering elements.

(4) Name and address of buyer

(5) In what form payment was received

(6) The guarantee on what is being ordered

(7) What sales tax (if any) was remitted

With these 7 *order elements* we can begin processing the order and computerize the data. Don't delay the order (provided that it is a valid one) waiting for all of the data processing to be completed. A typed shipping label should be immediately generated and the order promptly (within 48 hours, I believe) shipped.

If you rely on an outside computer service for data processing, you should deliver data to them on a regular basis. Once a week, or no less than twice per month (depending on your volume of business) is important. To make certain nothing is done in a helter-skelter fashion, specific dates (such as every Friday morning, or the first and fifteenth of each month) will work best.

In addition to processing all of your valuable data, you should also generate a set of labels from the most recent customers, for follow-up mailings. In addition to "package stuffers" (additional offers sent with the orders), it's a good idea to make a follow-up mailing to your new customers within 2 to 3 weeks from the date their order was shipped. They're still hot, and if they are happy with what you shipped, they're great candidates for additional business.

Only a handful of mail order sellers can make big money with "one-shot offers." 99% of us need repeat business to make our mail order ventures successful! Our goal is to entice each new customer into purchasing 2, 3, 4, 5 times, or more, before he or she, regretfully, no longer responds to our offers. And, our solid-gold customers are those who stick with us for many years, favoring us with many, many orders.

WHEN TO DROP A NAME
FROM YOUR CUSTOMER FILE

Any person who has not responded to our mailings for one full year (provided that we have sent them offers at least 4 times during a 12-month period) is no longer an active buyer. Before dropping customers from your master list of buyers, you will do well to make a special mailing to these people. Look over my sample *"I want to keep you as a customer* letter, and think about how you can adapt it to your use.

I am being very sincere when I state that I *do* regard my customers as mail order friends. We must do everything possible to keep these wonderful people thinking good thoughts about us. Our goal may be to sell to many thousands and thousands (perhaps even millions) of customers. Still, we must not lose sight of the fact that they are all individuals. They all want personal attention and service. Make certain your ads and mailings are as "personalized" as possible. Never write for a crowd of people, rather always use the personal one-to-one conversational approach.

THE STANDARD
DIRECT MAIL FORMAT

Your imagination is really your only limitation in designing a direct mail package. However, the following direct mail format has withstood the sands of time, and repeatedly proven itself to be effective in the majority of direct mail efforts.

Letters

1. First in importance in the direct format is the letter (remember: direct mail is supposed to be one-to-one, personal advertising). The letter can be one page or many pages. The key is to use as many words as needed

From the desk of

Russ von Hoelscher

A SPECIAL OFFER TO A FRIEND
I'VE MISSED HEARING FROM

Dear Friend,

I have always thought of the buyers of my books, manuals, reports and tapes to be my friends, even though I have only met a very small number of you in person. Even if you and I have never met, I want you to know that I consider you to be very special.

Our books and other materials are target-marketed to people who not only dream big dreams, but who are also willing to shut off the boob tube (at least some of the time) and get busy making their dreams a reality.

For twenty years I have been writing and publishing informative materials that help people help themselves. Many have written to me over the years, giving me credit for the great success they now enjoy. Although such beautiful letters make me suspender-popping proud, I really don't deserve this credit.

A teacher may have thousands of "students" over the years, and may do his darndest to help each one, but full credit for great achievements must go to those individuals who apply the knowledge they receive and carve out their own great measure of success.

The fact that several of my "friends and students" have surpassed me in the accumulation of wealth or other desirable achievements, brings me not a smidgen of resentment, but rather, so much pleasure.

We are all teachers and we are all students. Once we have the necessary "how to," we are only restricted by our imagination.

In looking over past records (in the mail order business this is an important task), I noted that we have not heard from you in over a year. The last thing I want to do is remove you from our mailing list of **treasured customers.** However, today postage and printing costs are at all-time highs. More than ever, it's important we send information on our business, investment and motivational offerings only to those who wish to receive them.

I sincerely hope that includes you.

George Allen, the highly regarded former professional football coach with the Washington Redskins and Los Angeles Rams, once said: "You die a little bit every time you lose a game."

I don't want to be overly dramatic, but I think I know what he meant. I don't want to lose you as a mail order friend and customer. To make it easy for you to send for some of our important new titles, I have enclosed a special *$5.00 Off Discount Coupon* in this envelope. The only stipulation is that you use it within the next 15 days to order items totalling $20 or more. That means up to a 25% savings for you.

Please look over the enclosed current brochure of new titles—truly our best selection ever—and consider how several of these items can help you reach personal achievement goals and financial independence.

Thanks for your consideration. I appreciate it. I

want your business, and guarantee to always try to please you.

You deserve Total Success,

Russ

Russ von Hoelscher

P.S. Although I'm hoping we'll have the privilege of receiving your order, you **can** remain on my special list without buying anything. If you're not ordering at this time, but want to remain on our mailing list to consider future offerings, please drop me a line and tell me to keep you on the list. That will please me. If you do favor us with your order now, you automatically stay on my "friend and customer" file.

Sample *"I want to keep you as a customer"* letter.

to sell your offer, but no more than necessary. Keep it friendly, personal, enthusiastic, with an easy to swallow hard sell, and *do* ask for the book order.

2. The standard and proven mailing piece consists of an outside envelope, letter, circular, order card and reply envelope.

3. All important sentences should be highlighted by bold type, caps, italics or underlining.

4. A two or four-page letter almost always has more pulling power than a one-page letter. In some cases (especially high-ticket newsletter subscription offers and home-study courses) extremely long letters (up to 8 pages and more) have proven themselves to be very, very effective. It's said, *Nobody has time to read long advertising sales letters, and yet they usually are the ones which bring home the most mail orders.* Think about it!

5. A neatly typed "personal style" letter is more effective than a professional-looking typeset letter. Everything in your letter should come across as one-to-one communication.

Circulars

1. A professional-looking circular (typeset with photos and/or art work) is usually the best way to support a personalized letter that contains no photos or art work.

2. The more expensive your offer is, the more professional-looking your circular (but not your letter) should be.

3. Use several "testimonials." If possible, use full names, because they are much more effective than the use of just initials.

Outside envelopes

1. While a combination of larger or smaller sizes of

envelopes have proven to be effective for various offers, the standard size No. 10 works best for most.

2. Teaser copy that relates to the copy inside usually, but not always, will increase response. Only individual tests will determine this.

Reply Envelopes

1. Any reply envelope increases results.

2. Postage-free reply envelopes will often out-pull those that require your customer to affix a stamp.

Order Card or Form

1. A separate order form will usually out-pull one that is printed on your circular that needs to be cut out.

2. An order form with an "official-looking" guarantee will usually out-pull one that simply states a guarantee.

Postage

1. Postage-metered envelopes will out-pull a pre-printed permit. Individual postage stamps slow down the mailing operation, but usually are most effective.

2. There is often little difference in pull between first class or bulk rate. However, if you use first class, always use a big, bold type to let the receiver know he is receiving a **FIRST CLASS** mailing. Never, never use a preprinted first class permit on your envelopes. If you do that, you are paying first class postage rates, while making your outer envelope appear to be a bulk-rate mailing. That's not being very smart.

My most important advice for your direct mail package (as it was in placing space ads) is to load up everything (the sales letter, the brochure or circulars, the lift letter—if you use one—and the order card) with

162

benefits, benefits, and still more benefits!

A LIFT LETTER
MAY LIFT RESPONSE

Many mail order companies have discovered a lift letter (a small, memo-sized letter, folded in half), can increase direct mail response. You've seen them hundreds of times. The folded-over message may say something like: "A message from Mr. Todd S. Blowhart, President of XYZ Company" or "Read this message only if you have decided *not* to order."

The small letter then opens to a brief message telling you several reasons why you should consider ordering (or reconsider your initial not to order decision).

The pitch usually includes restatement of the company's guarantee, and how this guarantee allows you to order without risk.

When the lift letter was first put into action several years ago, mailers reported excellent results and a big boost in responses. Today they are quite common, but they still can be effective and more than pay for themselves.

On some offers (when the dollar amount exceeds $40) I use them; on lower-priced offers I do not. When I *do* use them I generally take the positive approach. Frankly, I'm more than a little turned off by the often-used negative lift letter that begins, "Frankly, I'm puzzled." This type of lift letter goes on to state something to the effect: *Since our offer and guarantee is so superior, how can you possibly decide not to order? What's wrong with you?*

I don't like that condescending, negative style, and my intuition tells me many other potential buyers are also turned off by it.

I've had good success with a positive style approach that stresses benefits, and also tells potential responders to give me a call if they have questions they would like to ask.

I have reproduced one of my lift letters to give you an example of my approach:

ENCOURAGE PHONE CALLS AND PHONE ORDERS

It may be called by many of us *the mail order business*, but it's really *the direct response marketing business*. The mails may be our primary source to seek and receive business, but never underestimate the power of the telephone.

Many individuals and companies who did nearly 100% of their business exclusivey by mail, have turned to the telephone to dramatically increase their response.

Telemarketing is big business today, and it's going to get even bigger unless *rights of privacy* laws sweep the nation and put the lid on what has become a forceful marketing tool.

In your book or information by mail business, you may not employ advanced telemarketing techniques (although for some information sellers, this does work!) to solicit orders; however, you still should make good, profitable use of your telephone. Include your phone number in your mailings, and encourage folks to call you to ask questions or place orders. Don't be surprised if many who call with a question also place an order. It happens to me every single day.

I *want* people to call. I'll do my *best* to give them the answers they seek. Sure, I occasionally get calls from those few individuals who think I have nothing better to

ANY QUESTIONS OR DOUBTS?

...Inside is Russ von Hoelscher's personal message for you.

FROM THE DESK OF
Russ von Hoelscher

Dear Friend,

*My personal success philosophy is: **Don't give folks their money's worth**, **GIVE THEM MORE THAN THEIR MONEY'S WORTH**! Believe me, it's a way of life that pays rich rewards, and you can sleep good too.*

*I'm extremely proud of the fast-selling Profit Ideas hardcover books and our profitable "Fast Start" program. I hope you will join us now. I promise to do my best to make your success dreams come true. **This program really works!***

While I have done my best to fully describe this remarkable opportunity, I know you may still have questions you wish you could ask me...well now you can!

***Call me at (619) 560-6922 if you have any questions**. I want to help you make more money and reach your goals.*

Sincerely,

Russ

do with my time than to spend all afternoon giving them intensive phone lessons in successful direct response techniques. These are the same greedy people who offer to take me to lunch and then ask so many rapid-fire questions that I can't enjoy a single bite. I don't go to lunch with such people any more.

Once it's obvious that someone is unmercifully pumping me dry for free expertise, I simply inform them that my consultant's fee is a bargain at only $100 an hour—which it is. This always turns off the "free lunch" crowd and greatly benefits the select few who are most willing to pay for expert marketing advice.

We serve the needy—not the greedy. But any sincere person who has a question or two to ask about anything I may know, or am involved with, is encouraged to call me. No cost and no obligation!

I prefer a phone call that will usually take 10 minutes or less, to the time and effort involved in responding to individual questions by mail. I have also found that many of the good people who call seeking advice also favor us with their orders.

It's good business to be accessible, and willing to talk with people. Remember, the information by mail business is a communication business. Also, the person you take the time to help today, may be willing to help *you* with your problem tomorrow.

We are all teachers, and we are all students!

HOW TO GET
YOUR ENVELOPE OPENED

Today, a large number of people open their mail near a waste basket. Envelopes not perceived as valuable get deep-sixed! You may have a persuasive sales letter, an appealing brochure, and a great supportive cast of enclosures. Everything is just right to make people want

167

to rush to their nearest mailbox and send you their order once they've seen your offer. Still, this can't happen unless your outside envelope gets opened.

Here are 8 tips and techniques to entice those who receive your offer to open it and look at what's inside.

(1) Most people separate their daily mail into two categories. In one pile is the mail they "think" has value and perceive to be important. In the other pile is mail they consider to be less important, or worse yet, of no value at all. Many from this pile are thrown away unopened.

Most often the very best way to make your mailing appear to be very important is to make it look just like a personal letter. No teaser copy (claims typed or written on the outer envelope), nothing identifying you as a company trying to sell something. If your mailings go out in any way other than first class, don't advertise that fact. Use bulk rate stamps or a postage machine imprint. Never use a bulk rate indicia.

(2) The typing, handwriting or laser printing of addresses on envelopes may not be time-effective or cost-effective, but they will get more envelopes opened than those with mailing labels on them. If mailing labels must be used, make certain they are neat and not at all messy-looking.

(3) Window envelopes often get more attention than regular envelopes.

(4) Showing a facsimile check in a window envelope is an often-used direct mail tactic that seems to still work (even though I personally resent this ploy). The check, of course, represents a discount coupon, and not legal tender.

(5) Brief teaser copy sometimes will work well. Often brief bold command copy such as: **IMPORTANT— OPEN IMMEDIATELY,** gets the desired response.

(6) Predictions often work (when you're not using the personal touch). Using bold teaser copy to make several fearless predictions can arouse interest and the desire to open and learn more.

(7) Color and size can stimulate interest. Again, never to be used when trying to make your envelope look like personal mail. Bright-colored envelopes and/or large-size or unusually shaped envelopes are bound to be noticed and thereby invite opening.

(8) Teaser copy on the outside that declares a person has won a prize, or can obtain a free gift (keep in mind that you must deliver on such promises) get attention.

HOW TO OBTAIN TESTIMONIALS

Favorable testimonials from the media (newspapers, publications, TV, etc.) can give your book or other "paper and ink" product a big lift. However, several mail order information sellers operate in somewhat narrow markets that do not lend themselves to extensive media coverage.

That's no excuse not to actively seek favorable and reprintable comments from happy customers.

Most people—even those thoroughly pleased with your report or book—will not take the time to write and tell you so. That's just human nature. And that is why we must ask for what we want.

Here's 4 tips on how to secure valuable testimonials:

(1) When someone does write you a glowing letter that you would like to reprint, in part, in your advertising literature, write them and ask permission to do so. You need not use their full address, but a full name, plus city and state is desirable. Using initials only waters down the testimonial considerably. While the use

of a person's initials only after a solid testimonial is probably better than no testimonial at all, this approach leads to skepticism. If at all possible, you want the full name.

(2) You can include a note in your shipping package that encourages your customers to send their comments. You then seek permission to use the very best ones.

(3) You can even offer a "free gift" (perhaps a small booklet or short report, or an inexpensive office supply product) in return for comments.

(4) You can enclose a preprinted flyer that solicits comments and asks a few questions. This flyer plus the enclosure of a prepaid envelope will greatly increase written response.

In all cases, obtain signed permission before using your customers' comments in your ads or mailing pieces. You do not need permission to use comments or reviews from the media, because this is already considered a public statement.

WHAT YOU MUST KNOW WHEN CHOOSING MAILING LISTS

Before you rent or buy any mailing list for a direct mail campaign, you need to know the answers to the following 10 questions.

(1) Is this list a response or compiled list?

(2) Who are these people, and exactly what have they recently responded to?

(3) Is this a list of buyers or inquiries?

(4) How old is this list?

(5) What was the average dollar amount of their

recent purchase?

(6) Is a 60 to 120 day "hotline list" available?

(7) How many names are on the master list?

(8) How were the names obtained? (Space ads, direct mail, etc.)

(9) How have they paid for recent purchases? (By check, credit card, C.O.D. etc.)

(10) What are their demographics? (Sex, approximate age, income levels, etc.)

IMPORTANT POINT: The most responsive mailing list to use is usually made up of direct mail responders who have made a recent similar purchase from another company that was at the same, or greater amount than the price of your offer.

11 WAYS TO MAKE YOUR ORDER CARD SELL

(1) A separate order card usually outpulls one printed on a circular or brochure.

(2) Always use black ink.

(3) Card stock out-pulls plain paper.

(4) Color stock out-pulls plain white.

(5) It should be easy to read.

(6) It should contain the restatement of some primary benefit.

(7) It should restate your guarantee.

(8) It should tell the responder exactly what to do.

(9) It should state that you will ship promptly.

(10) It should be simple and easy to fill out.

(11) It should contain adequate space for the person to fill in his name and address (remembering that some people have long names and addresses), credit card information if offered, etc.

A REMINDER: Always enclose a return envelope.

YOU MUST ALWAYS TEST

There are so many variables (the headline, the overall advertising approach, the envelope, the price, etc.) in presenting your offer to potential mail order buyers. Only through testing can you establish your own best *control ads and mailing pieces.* And wise mail order operators always continue to test, always attempting to beat their own control, regardless of how profitable these ads or mail packages are. Only by constantly testing can we hope to (A) make it profitable and (B) make it even *more* profitable.

MAKE YOUR PROFITS RUN

Although it may be desirable (as mentioned previously), to continue to seek ways to improve even highly successful ads or mailings, I do not recommend radically changing something that is working well. You test in hopes to beat your control, but you never change your control until something better is proven.

The old stock market axiom: *Let your profits run, and cut your losses,* applies well to mail order advertising and promotion.

The strange truth is that many times a mail order operator will discontinue a proven successful ad or mailing after many months or years.

172

I must regretfully admit, in my early days in mail order marketing, I foolishly did this twice. I'll never make that mistake again, and I don't want you to do it even once. You may get tired of the same promotion and seek new challenges, but never, never, cease running an ad or making mailings that are profitable. Lack of sufficient response is the only reason to discontinue any form of advertising.

It's difficult enough to make any business profitable. Once it is working well and throwing off nice profits, NEVER turn off a *money machine*. Let your profits run!

Chapter 11

23 MASTER STEPS TO A MAIL ORDER DIRECT MARKETING FORTUNE

Let's summarize here, and present an overview of what you must become aware of, and do, if you desire success in the fascinating mail order information selling business.

(1) You need a game plan. Taking into account your initial budget, strengths and weaknesses, desires and goals, you should adopt both a short-range (3 to 6 month plan) and a longer range (6 month to 2 year) plan for your mail order information business. While it's quite likely that there will be changes made in your plans as you get deeply involved in your business, nevertheless, advance planning is important. And your objectives should be put on paper, black on white, not just stored in your memory. Written objectives and goals will help keep you on target. Constantly refer to them!

(2) You need your business tools. Your *business tools* include all of the office supplies and equipment that you will require. Space to conduct business. If you

175

will be home-based, seek some privacy in the house or apartment). A spare bedroom is ideal. Some have converted a corner of the garage into office space. The kitchen table has worked for many new information entrepreneurs, but hopefully, you can find a more suitable spot that offers more space and more privacy. A typewriter is a must, and so is a good file cabinet. If startup capital is modest, look for bargains on these and other essential needs at local thrift shops, Goodwill and Salvation Army stores.

A friend of mine recently bought a beautiful executive desk at a thrift shop for only $75. He showed me an office catalog that featured the same big desk for $595. If you look for bargains you will find them.

(3) Gather research and resource materials. The information business is a research business. In both preparing your products and sales literature, you'll be doing research and also need resource material. Buy books, subscribe to newsletters and magazines in your chosen field, start a "swipe file" that keeps you updated on the competition. Above all else, become familiar with vast storehouses of knowledge available at the biggest public library in your area.

(4) Seek expert advice. Unless you are making a very low-budget, shoestring start, it's wise to seek and pay for expert help. Attend seminars and workshops in your chosen information field; use the services of expert direct marketing copywriters and consultants, graphic artists, etc.

(5) Set up your record-keeping apparatus. Good records tell you where you are and where you're going. Ad-Lib Publications (P.O. Box 1102, Fairfield, IA 52556) has some excellent record-keeping manuals for publishers and mail order dealers.

(6) Choose your company name wisely. The name you hang on your fledgling new business can be a help or a hindrance. Think about it. Pick a business name

that makes a positive statement about you.

(7) Choose your "title" carefully. The title you give (if you are publishing your own materials) your book or report is extremely important. A good eye-catching title will help increase your sales.

(8) Sell related items. Whether you publish your own material, buy items for resale, or do some of both, make everything relate. This will encourage your customers to keep reordering, and that's the backbone of a successful mail order operation. As soon as possible a "catalog" should be produced (even if it's originally very simple and small) to maximize "bounce-back" and repeat ordering.

(9) Be a real professional. Sell only items you would appreciate owning at prices you would be willing to pay. Ship promptly. Use every legal ploy to get the business, and then offer the great service, information, and fairness, that will make them want to continue doing business with you.

(10) Be price conscious. Being price conscious means you both sell at the right price and buy (your printing, supplies, etc.) at the best price. Your goal is to buy low (without total disregard for quality) and sell high (obtain an excellent, yet fair price) on everything you market.

(11) Your media must be right for your "product" or vice versa. Is your product right for this market? Mail order advertising or direct mail success is obtainable only by matching our "paper and ink" product with the most likely potential market (the correct publications or best possible mailing lists). We may wish to test unfamiliar media on occasion, but most of our ad dollars should go into the likely media.

(12) Ads and mailing pieces must appeal to emotions and not intellect. Intelligence and knowledge are primarily responsible for advancement of the human race.

However, when it comes to most individual "buy or no buy" decisions, *feelings and emotions* usually are the prime motivators. Fact-filled copy alone won't get the job done. Emotional appeals, and the promise of personalized benefits, will up your response rate far more than ad copy that is purely logical.

(13) Use the K.I.S.S. approach. Our customers are definitely not stupid. Today's mail order responder is well-educated, well-informed, and knows exactly what he or she wants. While this is true, the *simple approach* still works best. Don't try to impress your audience with ten dollar words or high-brow conceptual advertising messages. Good advertising copy is always simple, sincere and direct. Keep everything easy to understand and very easy to place that order.

(14) Communicate one-to-one. Regardless if you're mailing only one mailing piece or mailing to one million people, a one-to-one personalized approach usually works wonders. I like to picture in my mind a single prospect, sitting next to me on a couch. To that one person (even if we're making a mass mailing or placing ads in high-circulation publications), I make my offer. In giving speeches to large audiences, and appearing on TV programs with hundreds of thousands watching, I learned this valuable lesson. *Whether the audience is large or small,* rave reviews only result from a sincere, open and personalized presentation. In mail selling, the personal approach brings the best response. We may use mass production, computers, countless lists of names of people we don't personally know, and lots of other mechanical, and unpersonal techniques to put our ad or brochure before Mr. John Smith. When he begins to read it, it's vital that our tone is personal, and that he can relate to and believe what we are telling him. Our only hope of receiving his precious response, is that in some way, he is touched by our personalized communication and claims.

(15) Fulfillment must run smoothly. Orders are processed and shipped promptly (within 48 hours of

receipt). If, for any reason an order must be delayed, a note to that effect is sent to our customer. On orders for substantial amounts, a "thank you" letter is sent. Obtaining orders puts you in business. Good fulfillment, record-keeping and data processing helps keep you in business.

(16) Stuffers are always enclosed to get cost-effective "bounce-back" orders. Bounce-back orders are very, very cost-effective, and should always be sought. To obtain them, you simply have your catalog, brochure or circulars included inside each order package you ship. You'll be amazed how many orders quickly *bounce back* to you.

(17) All new customers should quickly receive a follow-up mailing. Within 10 to 21 days of their initial order being shipped, each new customer should receive a follow-up mailing of other items you have for sale. *Get 'em while they're hot!*

(18) Learn as much as possible about individual "customer value." The average gross and net worth of each of our customers is extremely valuable information. We use it in decision-making on the cost and development of new customers and overall marketing strategy.

(19) Every offer you send must be loaded with "benefit copy." We think about and develop "you" copy, not "I" copy. We know who and what our potential mail order responders are most interested in and concerned about. Our advertising addresses the benefits they crave.

(20) Your customers are very special people and should be treated like royalty. Most successful mail order operations are very customer-satisfaction oriented. Our business stands or falls on how well we please our customers. We must entice them to stick with us and continue to order. To accomplish this, we must excel in service, as well as provide valuable information. It's

also a very good idea to be accessible and anxious to solve problems. Be helpful. *The more you give, the more you'll receive!*

(21) Stay in touch. No less than 4 mailings per year should be made to every person on our active customer file.

(22) Think Profits! Profitable mail order marketing is the result of profit-thinking and a willingness to test new ideas and concepts. We do not want to reinvent the wheel, so we *do* follow proven guidelines. At the same time, we invite our powerful Subconscious Mind to send us a stream of exciting new ideas concerning product development and creative marketing techniques. *Your thoughts can make you rich!*

(23) Think more profits! To ultimately make a fortune selling information by mail, first we strive to survive and make some profit. Then we strive to upgrade profits and beat our control. The difference between *getting by* and *getting rich* is **knowledge, desire, creative thought and persistence!** You've heard the old cliche: *a penny for your thoughts,* well, in this exciting business *your thoughts can make you a fortune!*

Chapter 12

PRODUCING AND SELLING OTHER BIG PROFIT PRODUCTS AND SERVICES

Up until now most of my attention has centered around "paper and ink" information products, although my advertising methods do relate to anything you may wish to sell by mail. Now let's look at some other related products that can be produced, packaged and sold by mail at big profits.

PROFESSIONAL SPEAKING: SEMINARS AND WORKSHOPS

My dear friend, world class professional speaker, Dottie Walters, is fond of saying "writers and publishers should also be speakers." How right she is!

If you package and sell information by mail, you're in the communication business. Why not consider also developing your topics into paid speeches, workshops or seminars? My pal, Al Galasso and I have taken

Dottie's advice and now produce popular Self-Publishing and Mail Order Success Seminars*, and they have become a great source of extra income.

Obviously, there is some real "personal fear" associated with standing up in front of people and speaking to them. Some experts claim it is one of man's greatest phobias. But it need not be. If the thought of speaking professionally has the butterflies in your tummy dancing in a mad orgy, get some help. If you know your subject matter well, and do not have a speech impediment, you can do it! Joining a local Toastmaster Club (found in hundreds of cities across the nation) is a great place to start. A Toastmaster Club is a group of men and women who gather on a regular basis (usually weekly) to help each other, in a supportive atmosphere, become better communicators.

I've been a Toastmaster for several years and without any reservations, I recommend this helpful organization to anyone. For the locations of clubs that meet in your area, write to the headquarters: Toastmasters International, 220 N. Grand Avenue, P.O. Box 10400, Santa Ana, CA 92711.

Another excellent, learn and earn source of professional speaking expertise is Dottie Walter's super news magazine, *Sharing Ideas,* and her highly-acclaimed six-tape album *How to Enter the World of Professional Speaking.* This incredible woman is a leading speaker, writer, publisher and booking agent. If you would like to make *money with your mouth* in addition to mail order, get in touch with her now: Dottie Walters, Royal Publishing, 18825 Hicrest Rd., P.O. Box 1120, Glendora, CA 91740.

---

*Write or call Al at American Book Exchange, P.O. Box 2525, La Mesa, CA 92041, concerning our next Self-Publishing or Mail Order Success Seminar.

CASSETTE AUDIO TAPES

Several years ago I realized increasing numbers of people were turning to cassette tapes for learning experiences. I wisely decided to include cassettes in my mix of products offered. It has paid off handsomely. I strongly suggest you, too, consider the many advantages of selling audio tape programs.

Here are just some of the valid reasons to sell audio tapes:

(1) Today there are over 100 million cassette tape players—in homes, offices and vehicles—a tailor-made market. Although music continues to dominate the audio cassette industry, increasing numbers of people are buying self-help and how-to tapes.

(2) Some people do little or no reading, but they haven't discontinued their desire to learn. A learning experience on tape is most desirable.

(3) Audio cassette tapes can be produced in modest quantities at very attractive prices, allowing you to enjoy substantial markups.

(4) Expert packaging of several tapes in one album, combined with written instructions (books, manuals, etc.), can produce a high-ticket "home study course" that can maximize your profits. Potential responders often have a "perceived dollar value" on individual items. However, by combining several items, including an attractive, large cassette tape album containing several tapes, you can often make a much higher combined price palatable.

Example: A New York information entrepreneur used to sell individual one-hour memory improvement audio tapes at $9.95 each. Sales were good, but profits were not sensational. Once he had a total of 8 different tapes, he decided to put them all in an attractive album.

He then published written instructions in a manual format. At his previous price of $9.95 each, 8 tapes were worth less than $80 retail. If he had sold the manual separately it would have been priced at about $20 per copy. However, he did not sell his tape album and manual package for less than $100; he successfully sold this combination package as a home study course for $179. *By combining several individual items into one big package, you can often increase your retail price. The sum total of the whole increases the perceived value of the individual components. Audio cassette tapes offer the information seller another rich avenue of profits. You should give audio tapes serious consideration.*

CASSETTE AUDIO TAPE
RECORDING & DUPLICATING

These firms can assist you in producing and/or duplicating cassette tapes for resale:

Business Cassette Prod.
P.O. Box 11338
Costa Mesa, CA 92627

*Mother Dubbers
13626 Gamma Road
Dallas, TX 75234

Books In Motion
E. 9212 Montgomery, Suite 504
Spokane, WA 99206

Alpha Omega
343 S. Madison Ave. Suite 17
Pasadena, CA 92201

VIDEO CASSETTE TAPES

Here's another rapid-growing industry that deserves our consideration. I don't have to tell you the video industry is booming today. Almost everyone either owns a VCR or is thinking seriously about getting one.

Much of what I've already told you about the positive side of audio tapes applies here. Mark-ups can be very

---

*Mother Dubbers also offers video services.

favorable, demand is increasing, etc. Unfortunately there is also some real roadblocks to producing and selling good how-to or self-help video tapes. Production costs are quite high to produce a video that is both interesting and informative. Any time you work with the visual medium, you have to be concerned with viewer interest.

I've personally switched off video tapes on subjects I like simply because they were boring. A man or woman constantly talking and using only a blackboard and signboards for props, just doesn't hold viewer attention. *The visual medium is an active medium.* To capture viewer interest you need multiple scenes, activity, a little humor, etc., to complement instructions. Video professionals can be hired to make it flow and come across stimulating, but it will cost money.

Don't produce a video cassette program unless you're convinced you have something unique that will sell, and then are willing and able to spend the effort and money to produce an interesting as well as informative tape. Presentation here is just as vital as content.

NEWSLETTERS

A newsletter can be a logical extension of your information by mail business. By first developing a market for books, reports and/or cassette tapes, a newsletter can provide a vehicle for continued sales and contact with your responders, as well as being a profit source by itself.

A newsletter can be launched as a primary mail sales objective, but to do this you must understand that you will earn little or no profits for at least the first year of operation. In most cases, you can expect to lose money for at least one year, and perhaps for two years.

If you're launching your information-by-mail business on a shoestring, you should not begin by publishing a newsletter.

By sticking to one well-defined field of interest and expertise with the manuals, books, and other items you sell, the publishing of a newsletter in this subject area may make sense once you have built up a good customer base. A mail order operator with even a small customer base—let's say only 5,000 buyers, but all in the same overall information category—could mail a newsletter subscription offer to this group of people of similar interests. If the newsletter goals were well-defined and the advertising was laden with beneficial copy, a good percentage of the 5,000 may subscribe. A 5% subscription response would give this new newsletter publisher a quick subscription base of 250 subscribers. From there the going would get tougher, as our newly established newsletter ventured outside the very responsive in-house mailing list and began using lists from other sources.

The thought of starting a newsletter *cold* doesn't turn me on unless big bucks will be available for a comprehensive *marketing attack*. Less money and less effort will be involved in using a customer base, all of whom share similar interests, to get a letter off the ground.

Chapter 13

AN INTERVIEW WITH MELVIN POWERS

As I neared completion of this manuscript, I began thinking about how helpful it would be to get some opinions on mail order and information marketing from another recognized expert. Immediately, my friend Melvin Powers came to mind. I phoned Melvin and he graciously agreed to an interview.

Melvin Powers has been in this business almost 40 years. He is a living legend in the mailorder and book-selling business. Another fellow publisher recently told me that I have now written and sold more books than the legendary Joe Karbo (although I'm quick to point out, I've yet to have one book sell as well as his mega-mail-order-seller, The Lazy Man's Way to Riches.) *With total sales approaching two hundred million copies, it's highly unlikely that I, or almost anyone else, will ever surpass the book sales of Mr. Powers. Read on—this man has some good information for you.*

RvH: How did you get started in the book and information business by mail order?

MP: I became interested in mail order when I was only sixteen years old. I always read many different magazines, and became fascinated with

189

the small classified ads that appeared in *Popular Science, Mechanics Illustrated,* and other such publications. In those early days I would respond to hundreds of different ads. I also would order every available book on the subjects of advertising, marketing and mail order. Soon I decided I wanted to sell books and booklets by mail. I liked the idea of selling information people wanted and would pay for.

RvH: Did you immediately become a self-publisher?

MP: No, during my first few years in this business, I bought books and booklets at wholesale prices from other publishers and offered them for sale by mail. In the beginning I worked with discounts of around 50% off, but once I started selling hundreds, then thousands of books, these publishers granted me much larger discounts.

RvH: Do you remember something about those early titles you purchased and then resold?

MP: They were booklets and books on astrology, magic, how to pass exams, how to play chess, a series of joke books, and other "how to" titles.

RvH: What was the secret to your immediate success?

MP: Choosing good titles and then writing good ads.

RvH: When did you decide to become a publisher?

MP: After two or three years of successfully selling books obtained from several other publishers, I decided to publish myself. I was deeply involved with magic, memory and hypnotism, all of which I incorporated into a stage act I performed at several clubs. The first books and booklets I published related to these subjects.

RvH: *Were your first publishing efforts successful?*

MP: Very successful! I developed a mail order catalog of interesting self-help titles, some of which I published, others which I obtained from other sources. By the time I was 21 years old, I was well established as a publisher and mail order book seller.

RvH: *As you look back, are you happy you chose this profession?*

MP: I love this business, Russ. It is a fascinating, creative business that has made so many of my dreams come true. I've made lots of money, and have had lots of fun, too. I intend to continue doing both.

RvH: *Do you consider the mail order self-help and information business of today to be as profitable as it has been in the past?*

MP: Absolutely! In fact, it's easier to make a fortune today than it was in the past. In addition to publications and direct mail, we now have other powerful media tools. Television marketing, for example, offers huge profits to today's mail order entrepreneur who will put books on cassette tapes, and offer a "package" of written and audio instructions. If you have a book, you should also produce tapes. This can greatly increase your potential profits. Of course, you must make a good presentation. The advertising is first in importance.

RvH: *In over 35 years of writing your own books, publishing them, and publishing hundreds of other books by various authors, plus selling books from other sources, do you have an idea of how many total books and booklets you have sold?*

191

MP: Close to two hundred million—a large percentage of which have been sold by mail!

RvH: *What has been your all-time, best-selling book?*

MP: I've published and sold over three million copies of *Psycho-Cybernetics,* by Dr. Maxwell Maltz. It's at the top of my best-selling list, and it still is selling. I've also published and sold over two million copies of Napoleon Hill's classic, *Think and Grow Rich.* Both of these great books have had a major impact on my life. I read *Think and Grow Rich* when I was a young man, and it convinced me I could achieve anything I wanted to achieve. I highly recommend both of these marvelous, self-enriching books. To be successful, a person must develop successful habits and think successfully.

RvH: *So very true. You have also authored several books. Which one has sold best?*

MP: *How to Get Rich in Mail Order* now has 300,000 copies in print, and continues to sell very well. I've also taken my own advice and produced audio cassette tapes. The book and audio tape album are currently a big hit on cable TV at about $150 per order.

RvH: *You started your mail order career by running small classified ads. I also got started this way, and continue to run them today. At the same time, we also do mass mailings, place large space ads, etc. Do you still use classifieds?*

MP: Yes. Like you, Russ, I'm involved in many marketing areas, but I still run those small ads. Some of the most successful and largest mail order companies: Mellinger, Charles Atlas, Specialty Merchandise Corporation, etc., have run classified ads with very few copy changes for decades. It still works!

RvH: What advice would you give a person who wants to get involved in the exciting and profitable mail order information business, but who has only a very limited amount of capital?

MP: This is one of the few business ventures that allows a person to get started without a lot of money. I would suggest a start-up that included a modest ad budget in the beginning,⋅and the sale of books available from other publishers. This works for many, and is exactly how I got started. Several publishers will sell to you wholesale, or dropship their books direct to their customers.

RvH: Any suggestions for the person who is determined to self-publish his or her own materials?

MP: Anyone who is going to get started publishing a book or booklet should start by producing it in the least costly format. It's a good idea to type the manuscript, run off a limited number of copies on a photo-copy machine, and bind it together with staples. This will keep production costs to a minimum. Once you're certain your ad is working well—and in mail order your ad will determine success or failure—you can overhaul your book and have it professionally typeset and printed in a more attractive format. First, discover if people will buy it! Test various ad copy.

RvH: Good advice. Years ago, ads could be run for books or manuals that were not even in existence. If the ad pulled well, the book was quickly written and published. When the ad flopped, the book idea was simply dropped. Today, however, the law says the product must be available before the ad is placed.

MP: That's right, Russ, but by using my low-budget publishing method, a person can test ads without putting large amounts of money into production.

RvH: You're right, advertising is the name of the mail order game. We rise or fall with the advertising we use. What advertising book has had the greatest influence on you, Melvin?

MP: There are many good books, that's why I strongly advise everyone who wants to get involved with mail order, to read dozens and dozens of mail order marketing and advertising books. My advice: buy all you can, and also check out and read everything available at a good public library. One of the best books on advertising is one that I publish, *How to Write a Good Advertisement,* by Victor O. Schwab.

RvH: That is an excellent book. It was written many years ago, but it has withstood the test of time. Do you have any more advice on mail order advertising?

MP: It's good mail order advertising sense to learn from those who are successful. Be a "copycat." Cut out and save successful ads from magazines, the ones that continue to appear, thus proving their value. Save the best direct mail packages, and also video tape the best offers that appear regularly on cable TV. Obviously you can't copy any of these word by word, but they can be a big help when you are preparing your own ads. Copy success!

RvH: What do you think are the important ingredients of a good ad copy?

MP: The headline, subheads, the overall benefits offered; all the vital things you teach, Russ. I also

---

How to Write a Good Advertisement, by Victor O. Schwab, is available for $21.00 postpaid from: Melvin Powers, 12015 Sherman Road, North Hollywood, CA 91605.

put great emphasis on the guarantee. The stronger it is the more it helps get the order. I was the first one to offer a 365-day guarantee. I also like Joe Karbo's approach concerning holding a responder's check for 30 days, promising to return it if the book does not meet expectations, and is returned. While only a small percentage will be returned, knowing one has this guarantee is reassuring. It definitely increases orders. I was also a pioneer in showing my bank deposits in my ads. This tells people they are dealing with someone who is successful.

RvH: *You're obviously very enthusiastic about the profit potential available through TV marketing. What about radio? Do you think it's a viable medium for today's mail order marketer?*

MP: Frankly, I've never made money with radio advertising. I'm convinced TV is where the action is.

RvH: *Any tips for selling books or other information products on television, with a limited budget?*

MP: Some cable TV stations make P.I. (Per Inquiry) deals. The stations run the ad spots at no charge, but require a percentage of every order received. This arrangement is ideal for the advertiser who has only a shoestring budget. Not all stations make these deals, but several do. It's a good idea to start seeking P.I. deals from cable stations in your immediate area. If they like what you wish to offer, they may be willing to accept a percentage of each order received (this can be 25% or more) as their payment.

RvH: *Some publications also make P.I. deals, usually splitting money received 50/50 with the publisher or mail order dealer. I'm sure you've made such arrangements. It's very cost effective, and can boost profits.*

MP: That's true. However, any print media that will offer P.I. advertising, usually is only interested in a deal that involves an item that is a proven winner. Once you have a strong order-pulling ad, it's possible to wheel and deal.

RvH: *I recommend that information marketers sell related materials from other publishers and also offer their items to other dealers. Do you share this advice?*

MP: Absolutely! You can multiply your sales by offering your publications to other mail order booksellers, catalog marketers, etc., and it's always good business for you to make additional sales by offering titles available from other publishers, as long as they grant you a decent discount of 100% or more. With drop-shipping, sales can be made without tying money up in inventory.

RvH: *Recently I've learned that you have become the owner of a restaurant in Los Angeles. You're not thinking of getting out of the mail order/ publishing business, are you?*

MP: Never! I love the mail order book business. My new Gorky's Restaurant, in partnership with my nephew, is a sideline business, but a very profitable sideline.

RvH: *Didn't anyone tell you, Melvin, over 80% of all restaurants fail?*

MP: That's true, Russ, just like the 80% or more who fail in mail order. Those statistics don't apply to the man or woman who is determined to make it and who prepares well for success. We went into the restaurant business without previous experience, and in less than one year, we have doubled the business. How did we do it? In addition to serving very good food, we applied sound marketing techniques. I read dozens of books on operating a restaurant. Good information on almost any business is available, but you must obtain it, read it, and then apply it if you want to enjoy the benefits.

RvH: *Excellent advice! I'm looking forward to visiting Gorky's, at 536 East Eighth Street in Los Angeles, and trust other readers of this book will do the same. Is there other advice you would offer the book and information mail order entrepreneur.*

MP: Believe in yourself, educate yourself, and know you can be successful. Don't listen to the majority of people, even friends or relatives, who are negative. Politely walk away when people start telling you, "You can't do that," or "This won't work," etc. Listen to and learn from positive, successful people who have the "I can" and "you can" attitude. Learn more so you can earn more. Read everything available on the subjects you're involved with or wish to become involved in. Start by reading all of Russ von Hoelscher's informative books.

RvH: *Thanks for so much good advice, Melvin, and for the plug. I appreciate the time you have shared. I know your remarks will be extremely helpful to all readers of this book. You have written and also published so many excellent books. For starters, I recommend that everyone order your How to Get Rich in Mail Order, and How to Write a Good Advertisement" by Victor Schwab.*

Section III
SOURCE DIRECTORY

VITAL

SOURCES

Here is a *Source Directory* of vital information for anyone who wants to sell books and information by mail successfully.

SOURCE DIRECTORY
TABLE OF CONTENTS

IMPORTANT HOW-TO BOOKS AND TAPES FOR PUBLISHERS

The Lazy Man's Way to Riches, by Joe Karbo. Legendary Joe Karbo passed away several years ago, but this bestseller (one of the all-time best-selling mail order books) continues to bring in those $10 orders! An "instant success" since Joe self-published it early in the 1970s, it remains important reading for all mail order operators. Mr. Karbo was a mail order advertising and promotion genius. Your author once asked Joe Karbo in the mid 1970s if he really believed mail order was an easy, lazy man's business. His answer was, and is, thought-provoking: *"It's easy when you make it work to make it work right, you need to do a great deal of creative thinking.* How right he is! As a tribute to his genius and success, his famous space ad used to sell this book is among the most imitated in mail order circles. If you don't own a copy of this book, why not send for it now! You know the price, $10 postpaid from: Financial Publishers, 17105 South Pacific, Sunset Beach, CA 90742.

How to Sell Books by Mail and *Directory of Wholesale Book Sources,* by Joseph S. Soukup. Another great manual plus source directory for anyone interested in selling books by mail. Easy to read and easy to use. Order both for only $11.00, postpaid from PROFIT IDEAS, 254 E. Grand Ave., Escondido, CA 92025.

How to Get Rich in Mail Order by Melvin Powers. My friend Melvin is a respected pioneer and leader in the *how-to* and self-help publishing movement. In addition to writing, publishing and selling millions of his own books, he has published and sold many millions of books for other authors. In this classic mail order business book, he shares his vast storehouse of experience. The book is jam-packed full of solid *how-to* information. *How to choose your topic; how to write good response ads; how to get the most from your advertising dollar, plus much more, including how to get very rich.* Truly a "must own" manual. Yours for $20 plus $2.00 postage from: Melvin Powers, 12015 Sherman Rd., North Hollywood, CA 91605.

How to Self-Publish Your Book and Have the Fun and Excitement of Being a Best-selling Author, by Melvin Powers. This is the ideal companion volume to the author's mega best-seller, *How to Get Rich in Mail Order*. Melvin knows how to write and/or publish books, and then sell them by the millions! In the arena of self-publishing and mail order book and manual selling, Mr. Powers is a superstar. This book offers the standard self-publishing instructions (how to choose a topic, copyright information, etc.) plus plenty of really creative and insightful advice from a real pro. A bargain at just $10 plus $1 postage from: Melvin Powers, 12015 Sherman Rd., North Hollywood, CA 91605.

Dialing For Dollars, by Eileen and T.J. Rohleder. This revolutionary, one-of-a-kind manual has flung open the door of vast opportunities to publishers and mail order book and booklet sellers. Sharp entrepreneurs are making up to $1,000 a day, and in some cases, even more. You profit by receiving phone calls. Best of all, you never have to talk to anyone! The Rohleders have created and fine-tuned a system that allows you to use a simple telephone answering machine, or a digital voice mailbox, which does the book selling for you! Believe me, the Rohleder money-making system is simple, powerful and extremely profitable. You can use this system to sell your own books, manuals, booklets or reports, and/or you may want to sell the impressive line of manuals published by T.J. and Eileen. First of all, you need to order *Dialing for Dollars*. This fantastic manual reveals secrets that allowed the Rohleders to go from a small investment (well under $1,000), to over three million dollars in sales in less than two years. Yes, that is the gospel truth! As their marketing consultant and advertising copywriter, I've seen (and helped produce) the amazing rags-to-riches results. You need this super manual, and I've got them ready to ship by fast first class mail. To get your copy, send $23 ($20 plus $3 for first class delivery), to Publishers Media, Dept. DFD, P.O. Box 546, El Cajon, CA 92022.

The Self-Publishing Manual, by Dan Poynter. I've known Dan over 10 years and I respect his talent and professionalism. This book is a highly recommended short course in writing, publishing and selling your own books. Don't even consider self-publishing your own book until you own and have read this informative guide book cover to cover. The new third revised 352-page softcover edition is now available. $14.95 plus $1.00 postage/handling from: Para Publishing, P.O. Box 4232, Santa Barbara, CA 93101.

Writer's Utopia Formula Report, by Jerry Buchanan. My friend Jerry is the *great grandfather* of the *information by mail order business.* He is a real pro who has helped a great many enterprising men and women get started right. His W.U.F.R. book is fun to read and loaded with the money-making tips, tricks and professional techniques of a man who teaches from experience, not from a textbook. $10 plus $2 postage will get your copy delivered from: Towers Club, U.S.A., P.O. Box 2038, Vancouver, WA 98661.

How to Make Money Writing at Home, by Steve Lockman. This is a complete career manual that will get you started making money as a freelance writer from the comfort of your own home. You can make money, without previous experience, in several high-paying markets: the greeting-card market, writing for children, comedy, resume service writing, business and advertising copywriting, plus much more. You'll even learn how to write full-length books, and how to effectively advertise your writing service. Order this unique manual for only $14.95 (and that includes first class mail delivery) from the author: Steve Lockman, Rt. 1, Box S, Lancaster, MN 56735.

The Unabashed Self-Promoters Guide, by Dr. Jeffrey Lant. Subtitled: *What Every Man, Woman, Child and Organization in America Needs to Know About Getting Ahead by Exploiting the Media.* This is a totally unique, "must own" rare and valuable book. I think any publisher and/or mail order book seller large or small, who does not buy it, read it, and use its illuminating contents, is very foolhardy. This is the best book on the vital subject of low-cost, high-exposure self-promotion. You will learn the prerequisites for totally successful self-promotion, how to approach the media, how to put together your own dazzling media kit, plus much more. The price for Dr. Lant's large 8 1/2 x 11 softback manual is $30, plus $2.50 for postage/handling from: Publishers Media, Dept. USP, P.O. Box 546, El Cajon, CA 92022.

The Self-Publishing Success Tapes, by Russ von Hoelscher and Al Galasso. Six audio cassette tapes (six hours of powerful instructions) on how to write, publish and profitably market your own books, manuals, booklets, and/or audio or visual tapes. Here are just some of the vital topics expertly covered: how to know what your chances for success will be, *before* you begin your project; how to use the powerful "simplified" method to write booklets, reports, or even full-size books quickly and expertly, even if you have no previous writing experience; how to get thousands of dollars worth of free publicity; low-cost, high-impact advertising techniques; how to write effective marketing documents—ads, brochures, sales letters, etc.; where to find a never-ending stream of topics that people are clamoring for. All this and much more, including the secrets of success by ten of today's richest self-publishers, how to inexpensively copyright everything you produce, plus how to obtain "outside capital" for your self-publishing project. It's all here in the "Self-Publishing Success Tapes." Everything you must know if you want to self-publish yourself to super success. Six hours of step-by-step professional guidance by two leaders in this exciting field. Six cassette tapes in a beautiful album, for only $59.95. And that price includes first class delivery. Order from: Publishers Media, Dept. SPT, P.O. Box 546, El Cajon, CA 92022.

How to Get a Credit Card Merchant's Account, by Russ von Hoelscher. Learn how you can get set up to accept VISA/Mastercard orders by phone and/or mail. Increase your business up to 100% without spending more on advertising. Only $6.00 from Publishers Media, P.O. Box 546, El Cajon, CA 92022.

How to Make a Fortune in the Pay-Per-Call Telephone Information Business. This is red-hot inside information on the exploding 900 phone business. If you want to start making $$$—get this report today for only $6.00. SPECIAL OFFER: Order *How to Get a Credit Card Merchant's Account* and *How to Make a Fortune in the Pay-Per Call Telephone Information Business* for only $10. Both reports will be rushed to you by fast first class mail. Order from Publishers Media, Dept. R, P.O. Box 546, El Cajon, CA 92022.

OTHER IMPORTANT BUSINESS BOOKS AND MANUALS

The Honest to Goodness Get Rich Quick Book, by Russ von Hoelscher. The title is not the only thing that's sensational about this one-of-a-kind new book. Hundreds of profit-producing tricks, techniques and sure-fire strategies, plus 15 master plans that show you how to make big money in a hurry! A steal at only $12 plus $2 postage/handling from: Profit Ideas, 254 E. Grand Ave., Escondido, CA 92025.

Tricks of the Trade, by Dr. Jeffrey Lant. Newly published, this is the latest volume in my friend Jeffrey's nationally acclaimed "Get Ahead" series which continues to provide the kinds of specific and detailed information people want and need to create profitable part- and full-time information and advice businesses in any field. You'll learn: The 8-part Problem-solving Process, the backbone of any advisor's practice; The 10-Step Mobile-Mini Conglomerate, a wealth-producing machine that shows advisors how to benefit from what they know and can do through a series of problem-solving formats, including direct one-on-one advising, retainer contracts, talk programs, audio and video cassettes, booklets and books, etc., plus much more.

This is a big (8 1/2 x 11) soft-cover manual, loaded with vital wealth-building information. $30 plus $2.00 postage/handling from: Publishers Media, Dept. TOT, P.O. Box 546, El Cajon, CA 92022.

Small-Time Operator, by Bernard Kamoroff, C.P.A. This is one of the finest books ever written and published on the "Mechanics" of running a successful, small business. *How to get started right and stay on target; how to set up your books and record-keeping system; how to deal effectively with employees; handle your tax responsibilities, and a whole lot more.* The subject matter may appear dull, albeit necessary, but Mr. Kamoroff has accomplished the ultimate for a book of this nature. His information is crucial, and his writing style makes it come to life and capture our interest. Only $14.95 plus $2.00 from: Bell Springs Publishing, P.O. Box 640, Laytonville, CA 95454.

IMPORTANT DIRECTORIES

Directory of Leading Magazines and Newspapers. A great source of approximately 300 U.S. newspapers and almost 600 most popular consumer and trade magazines. Names, addresses and current circulation. Whether for advertising purposes or as a source of free publicity, this new directory will help you reach millions of buyers for any product, service or book you wish to promote. Only $12 postpaid from: Publishers Media, Dept. DOL, P.O. Box 546, El Cajon, CA 92022.

Book Dealers Dropship Directory, by Al Galasso. Dropshipping enables you to sell books, collect payment in advance, then have the books shipped direct to your customers from the prime source. You carry no inventory. This directory lists hundreds of reliable dropship publishers. A great source guide! Order now for only $10.00 postpaid from: American Bookdealers Exchange, Box 606, Cottage Grove, OR 97424.

The Directory of Wholesale Printing and Office Supplies. You can slash up to 50% off your printing and office supply costs by securing a copy of the latest edition of "Directory of Wholesale Printing and Office Supply Sources." This super directory is loaded with great wholesale sources that can save you a bundle on office supplies and mail order printing. Only $9.95 postpaid from: A.I.M., Dept. WP, P.O. Box 22822, San Diego, CA 92192.

SPECIAL PUBLICATION OFFERS

Publishers Media (P.O. Box 546, El Cajon, CA 92022) has many back issues of Russ von Hoelscher's *Freelance*, and *Words for Wealth* newsletters available. Good information for mail order booksellers and/or anyone thinking about self-publishing a book or manual. Special! 6 back issues (a reg. $18 value) for only $5 postpaid.

Book Dealers World is the Direct Mail Marketplace for Book Dealers, Writers, Dropshippers, and Independent Publishers. Each issue is loaded with valuable publishing-book selling information from editorial director Al Galasso, and many of today's most creative minds, including: Dr. Jeffrey Lant, Cynthia Schubert, Bev Harris, David Bendah and Russ von Hoelscher. This is a most worthwhile publication. Just $3.00 will get you a sample copy from: North American Bookdealers Exchange, P.O. Box 606, Cottage Grove, OR 97424.

International Wealth Success is a unique mail order monthly business opportunities newsletter covering capital sources, finder's fees, real estate, getting started in mail order, import-export quick methods for raising money, venture capital, etc. Subscribers are entitled to run 12 free ads per year in the newsletter. Every issue is at least 16 pages and includes real-life experiences from Beginning Wealth Builders who are making their fortune today. Sample copy only $2.00. I.W.S., Inc., 24 Canterbury Rd., Rockville Centre, NY 11570.

Sharing Ideas, is a very special news magazine published by our friend, world-class professional speaker, Dottie Walters. Dottie shows writers/publishers how they can make lots of extra money in the fascinating world of speaking for pay. Each big (up to 48 pages or more) issue is crammed with vital information, and this lively publication is as entertaining as it is informative. A sample copy is only $5.00 from: Royal Publishing, 18825 Hicrest Rd., P.O. Box 1120, Glendora, CA 91740. (Author's note: when you send for a sample of Dottie's splendid news-magazine, she will enclose free information on her highly recommended cassette tape album, *How to Enter the World of Professional Speaking.)*

MAIL ORDER AND PUBLISHING NEWSLETTERS/MAGAZINES

Write them for more information

Direct Response
Profit Report
P.O. Box 546
El Cajon, CA 92022
Sample copy, $3

Opportunity Magazine
73 Spring St.
New York, NY 10012
Sample copy, $2

Book Dealers World
P.O. Box 606
Cottage Grove, OR 97424
Sample copy, $3

Towers Club Newsletter
P.O. Box 2038
Vancouver, WA 98668
Sample copy, $3

Small Press Review
P.O. Box 100
Paradise, CA 95969
Sample copy, $2

Alps Monthly
P.O. Box 99394
San Francisco, CA 94109
Sample copy, $1

The Huenefeld Report
P.O. Box U
Bedford, MA 01730
Sample copy, $6

Direct Response Specialist
P.O. Box 1075
Tarpon Springs, FL 34286
Sample copy, $3

Direct Marketing Magazine
224 Seventh St.
Garden City, NY 11530
Sample copy, $5

DM News
19 W. 21st St.
New York, NY 10010
Sample copy, FREE

Spare Time Money-
    Making Opportunities
5810 W. Oklahoma Ave.
Milwaukee, WI 53219
Sample copy, $2

Cosmep Newsletter
P.O. Box 703
San Francisco, CA 94101
Sample copy, FREE

PROFESSIONAL WRITING/ PUBLISHING/BOOK SELLING ORGANIZATIONS

American Bookseller Assoc.
122 E. 42nd St.
New York, NY 10168

Cosmep
P.O. Box 703
San Francisco, CA 94101

American Bookdealers
    Exchange
Box 606
Cottage Grove, OR 97424

Independent Publishers
Network
P.O. Box 546
El Cajon, CA 92022

American Library Assoc.
50 E. Huron St.
Chicago, IL 60611

Marin Self-Publishers Assoc.
P.O. Box 343
Ross, CA 94957

The Authors Guild
234 W. 44th St.
New York, NY 10036

The National Writers Club
1450 So. Havana, No. 620
Aurora, CO 80012

Book Publicists of So. Calif.
6430 Sunset Bl., No. 503
Hollywood, CA 90028

Publishers Marketing Assoc.
P.O. Box 299
Hermosa Beach, CA 90254

MAIL ORDER BOOK PUBLISHERS

These leading publishers and major distributors offer book selling programs, wholesale prices, and/or dropshipping on many different titles.

Profit Ideas
254 E. Grand Ave.
Escondido, CA 92025

Premier Publishers, Inc.
Box 330309
Ft. Worth, TX 76163

American Bookdealers
    Exchange
Box 606
Cottage Grove, CA 97424

Wilshire Book Co.
12015 Sherman Road
North Hollywood, CA 91605

Selective Books, Inc.
P.O. Box 1140
Clearwater, FL 33517

Stew Caverly
216 McLean St.
Wilkes-Barre, PA 18702

Cuppett Enterprises
P.O. Box 91
Wilmington, CA 90748

M.O.R.E.
305 E. Main St.
Goessel, KS 67053

Jeffrey Lant, Assoc.
50 Follen St., Ste. 507
Cambridge, MA 02138

Mitchell Enterprises
204 Oakdale
Pasadena, TX 77506

ARCO Publishing Co.
215 Park Ave., South
New York, NY 10003

SELECT MAJOR BOOK PUBLISHERS

In addition to being a wholesale source of nonfiction titles, you may wish to request to be put on their mailing list to buy discontinued titles

Simon & Schuster
1230 Ave. of the Americas
New York, NY 10020

McGraw-Hill Book Co.
1221 Ave. of the Americas
New York, NY 10020

Fleming Revell Co.
Central Ave.
Old Tappan, NJ 07675

W.W. Norton Co., Inc.
500 5th Ave.
New York, NY 10110

Farnsworth Publishing Co.
78 Randall Ave.
Rockville Centre, NY 11570

William Morrow & Co.
105 Madison Ave.
New York, NY 10016

Addison-Wesley Pub. Co.
Jacob Way
Reading, MA 01867

Dell Publishing Co., Inc.
1 Dag Hammarskjold Plaza
New York, NY 10017

Nelson-Hall Publishers
111 North Canal St.
Chicago, IL 60606

Lyle Stuart Inc.
120 Enterprise Ave.
Secaucus, NJ 07094

St. Martin's Press
175 5th Ave.
New York, NY 10010

Doubleday & Co., Inc.
245 Park Ave.
New York, NY 10167

Harper & Rowe Books
10 E. 53rd St.
New York, NY 10022

Prentice-Hall, Inc.
Business Book Division
Englewood, NJ 07632

Random House, Inc.
201 E. 50th St.
New York, NY 10022

Charles Scribner & Sons
866 3rd Ave.
New York, NY 10022

Little, Brown & Co.
34 Beacon St.
Boston, MA 02108

SOURCES FOR CLOSEOUT AND REMAINDER BOOKS

Book World Promotions, Inc.
87-93 Christie St.
Newark, NJ 07105

Outlet Book Co.
225 Park Ave., South
New York, NY 10016

S&L Sales
P.O. Box 2067, Ind. Blvd.
Waycross, GA 31501

Overstock Book Co.
120 Secatogue Ave.
Farmingdale, NY 11735

Publishers Marketing Enter.
386 Park Ave., South
New York, NY 10016

Western Book Distributors
2970 San Pablo Ave.
Berkeley, CA 94702

BOOK & MANUAL PRINTERS

Kingsport Press, Inc.
P.O. Box 711
Kingsport, TN 37662

McNaughton & Gunn, Inc.
P.O. Box M-2060
Ann Arbor, MI 48106

R.R. Donnelly & Sons
2223 Martin Luther King Dr.
Chicago, IL 60616

Book-Mart Press, Inc.
2001 Forty-Second St.
North Bergen, NJ 07047

Interstate Book Mfg.
2115 E. Kansas City Rd.
Olathe, KS 66061

Delta Lithograph Co.
14731 Califa St.
Van Nuys, CA 91411

Bookmasters
P.O. Box 159
Ashland, OH 44805

Book Press
Putney Road
Brattleboro, VT 05301

Griffin Printing
544 W. Colorado St.
Glendale, CA 91204

KNI, Inc.
1240 S. State College Bl.
Anaheim, CA 92806

Eerdman's Printing Co.
231 Jefferson Ave., S.E.
Grand Rapids, MI 49503

Braum-Brumfield, Inc.
P.O. Box 1203
Ann Arbor, MI 48106

Thompson-Shore, Inc.
7300 W. Joy St.
Dexter, MI 48130

Maverick Publications
P.O. Box 243
Bend, OR 97701

Apollo Books, Inc.
107 Lafayette St.
Winona, MN 55987

George Banta Co.
Menasha, WI 54942

MULTI-PURPOSE
OFFSET PRINTERS

To print circulars, brochures, letterheads.
They also can print booklets, reports, and directories.

Henry Birtle Co.
1143 E. Colorado St.
Glendale, CA 91205

Big City Litho
550 N. Claremont Blvd.
Claremont, CA 91711

Speedy Printers
23800 Aurora Rd.
Bedford Hts., OH 44147

M.O.R.E. Printing
307 E. Main St., Dept. R
Goessel, KS 67053

Equitable Web Offset
24 New Bridge Rd.
Bergen Field, NJ 07621

Fitch Graphics
P.O. Box 768500
Atlanta, GA 30328

Dinner & Klein
600 S. Spokane St.
Seattle, WA 98124

Econo-Printers
11565 Ridgewood Circle N.
Seminole, FL 33542

Creative Printing
309 S. Third St.
Ironton, OH 45638

Robeson Press
P.O. Box 130
Pembroke, NC 28372

Mark's Printing Service
P.O. Box 308
McKeesport, PA 15134

Classic Printing Co.
7250 Auburn Bl. Suite 143
Citrus Heights, CA 95610

Dress America, Inc.
1001 Nicholas Bl.
Elk Grove Village, EL 60007

Two Brothers, Inc.
1602 Locust St.
St. Louis, MO 63103

G&G Press
P.O. Box 660813
Miami, FL 33266

FULL COLOR PRINTERS

For full color brochures, flyers, catalog sheets, etc.

Volkmuth Printers, Inc.
East Hwy. 23, Box 1007
St. Cloud, MN 56302

Brown Printing Co.
U.S. Hwy. 14, West
Waseca, MN 56093

The Press
18780 W. 78th St.
Chanhassen, MN 55317

Direct Press Modern Litho
386 Oakwood Rd.
Huntington Station, NY 11746

Combo Color Co.
50 Madison St.
Maywood, IL 60153

Petty Co.
41 E. 42nd St.
New York, NY 10017

WEB PRINTERS

*Their specialty is long runs, often produced on low-cost newsprint.
Tabloids, brochures, newspapers, etc.*

Western Offset
348 W. Market St. #206
San Diego, CA 92101

Pomerado Publishing Co.
13247 Poway Rd.
Poway, CA 92064

Western Web Printing
4005 S. Western Ave.
Sioux Falls, SD 57101

Des Plaines Publishing Co.
1000 Executive Way
Des Plaines, IL 60018

Econo Printers
11565 Ridgewood Circle N.
Seminole, FL 33542

Sun Litho
7950 Haskell Ave.
Van Nuys, CA 91406

ENVELOPE MANUFACTURERS /PRINTERS

Continental Envelope Corp.
5515 Shore Trail NE
Prior Lake, MN 55372

Golden State Envelopes
1601 Gower St.
Los Angeles, CA 90028

Gotham Envelope Corp.
1 Madison St.
East Rutherford, NJ 07073

Accurate Envelope Co., Inc.
320 Lafayette St.
New York, NY 10012

Transco Envelope Co.
3542 N. Kimball Ave.
Chicago, IL 60618

U.S. Envelope
349f West Tremont St.
Charlotte, NC 28203

Gilmore Envelope Co.
4540 Worth St.
Los Angeles, CA 90023

Ohio Envelope
5161 W. 164th St.
Cleveland, OH 44142

Triangle Envelope Co.
61 Visco Court
Nashville, TN 37210

Glendale EnvelopeCo.
634 West Broadway
Glendale, CA 91204

Design Distributors Inc.
45 E. Industry Ct.
Deer Park, NY 11729

Mail-Well Envelope Co.
809 W. Santa Anita St.
San Gabriel, CA 91778

Envelopes Limited
899 E. 1st St.
Kansas City, MO 64106

Southwest Envelope Co.
3839 N. 35th St.
Phoenix, AZ 85017

Rockmont Envelope Co.
360 W. Burgatti St.
Salt Lake City, UT 84115

LOW-COST
COLOR SEPARATIONS

These firms prepare color photos for printing.

National Laser Separations,
Inc.
3501 N.W. 67th St.
Miami, FL 33147

Toucan Scan
407 N.W. 16th Ave.
Portland, OR 97209

TYPESETTING

Ashley Advertising, Inc.
P.O. Box 20822
Portland, OR 97220

TYPING SERVICES

Steve Lockman
P.O. Box 137
Lancaster, MN 56735

Mailathon, Inc.
16 Van Wetering Pl.
Hackensack, NJ 07601

MAILING LIST BROKERS

List World
555 Sparkman, #208, Rm. 17
Huntsville, AL 35816

Ed Burnett
99 W. Sheffield Ave.
Englewood, NJ 07631

Action Markets
1710 Highway 35
Ocean, NJ 07712

Trade Winds Marketing
31 Tracy Rd.
New Paltz, NY 12561

Hugo Dunhill Mailing Lists
630 Third Ave.
New York, NY 10017

Action Markets
1710 Highway 35
Ocean, NJ 07712

Enterprise Lists
725 Market St.
Wilmington, DE 19801

AIM Lists
P.O. Box 22822
San Diego, CA 92192

Hank Marshall
P.O. Box 2729
Laguna Hills, CA 92653

Accredited Mailing Lists Inc.
5272 River Rd.
Washington, DC 20016

COMPUTER SERVICES

Speedata Ltd.
1200 Shames Dr.
Westbury, NY 11590
(516) 997-8881

CCX
301 Industrial Bl.
Conway, AR 72032
(501) 329-6836

Hallmark Data Systems, Inc.
5500 Touhy Ave.
Skokie, IL 60077
(312) 674-6900

Adoniram
P.O. Box 786
Ft. Worth, TX 76101
(817) 589-7657

Data Services
49 Valley
Furlong, PA 18925
(215) 343-6166

AFC Computed Services
370 Seventh Ave.
New York, NY 10001
(212) 564-6400

New Processing Corp.
7650 E. Redfield Rd., Ste. 2
Scottsdale, AZ 85260
(602) 483-2600

Printronic Corp.
10 Columbus Circle
New York, NY 10019
(212) 247-8800

Creative Mailings, Inc.
20850 Leapwood, Stes. C&E
Carson, CA 90746
(213) 532-8296

MS Data Service Corp.
10221 Slater Ave., No. 112
Fountain Valley, CA 92708
(714) 962-8863

Mailing Data Services, Inc.
510 E. Commercial St.
Los Angeles, CA 90012
(213) 626-6301

Anchor Computer
750 Zeckendorf Bl.
Garden City, NY 11530
(212) 695-3600

EnertexComputer Concepts
444 Park Ave., S.
New York, NY 10016
(212) 685-3535

DM Data Services
814 Eagle Dr.
Bensenville, IL 60106
(800) 828-7527

COMPUTER SUPPLIES

Devoke Data Products
1500 Martin Ave.
Santa Clara, CA 95050

MISCO
One Misco Plaza
Holmdel, NJ 07733

Mail Advertising Supply Co.
P.O. Box 363
Waukesha, WI 53187

Executive Computer Supplies
P.O. Box 5153
Largo, FL 33540

GRAPHIC ART SUPPLIES

Graphic Products Corp.
3601 Edison Pl.
Rolling Meadows, IL 60008

Dot Pasteup Supplies
1612 California St.
Omaha, NE 68102

Midwest Publishers Supply
4640 N. Olcott Ave.
Chicago, IL 60656

Hartco Products
West Jefferson, OH 43162

FREE-LANCE GRAPHIC ARTISTS

Gray Studios
P.O. Box 811 –26
Levittown, PA 19058

CLIP ART

Art Master
500 N. Claremont Bl.
Claremont, CA 91711

Dynamic Graphics
6000 N. Forest Park Dr.
Peoria, IL 61656

Creative Media
P.O. Box 5955
Berkeley, CA 94705

Volk Clip Art
Pleasantville, NJ 08232

A.H. Gaebel, Inc.
P.O. Box 5
East Syracuse, NY 13057

Graphics Master
P.O. Box 46086
Los Angeles, CA 90046

BUSINESS FORMS

Amsterdam Printing & Litho
Amsterdam, NY 12010

McBee Mail Order Forms
299 Cherry Hill Rd.
Parsippany, NY 07054

Streamliners
P.O. Box 480
Mechanicsburg, PA 17055

Pickett-Chartpak
One River Road
Leeds, MA 01053

OFFICE SUPPLIES & PRODUCTS

Viking Office Products
13515 S. Figueroa St.
Los Angeles, CA 90061

Business Envelope Manuf.
900 Grand Bl.
Deer Park, NY 11729

Grayarc
P.O. Box 2944
Hartford, CT 06104

National Pen Corp.
9395 Cabot Dr.
San Diego, CA 92181

The Stationery House
1000 Florida Ave.
Hagerstown, MD 21741

NEBS
500 Main St.
Groton, MA 01470

The Drawing Board
P.O. Box 220505
Dallas, TX 75222

JEFFCO Inc.
205 Hallock Ave.
Middlesex, NJ 08846

Quill Corp.
100 S. Scheiter Rd.
Lincolnshire, IL 60198

SPECIALTY BOOK/
OFFICE SUPPLIES & EQUIPMENT

Book Bins, Wire Book Easels,
Book Display Racks, etc.:

The Highsmith Co., Inc.
P.O. Box 800B
Highway 106 East
Ft. Atkinson, WI 53538
(800) 558-2110

Wire Literature Holders
Pegboards, Display Racks:

Siegel Display Products
P.O. Box 95
Minneapolis, MN 55440
(612) 349-1493

Shipping Bags, Mailing Bags,
Literature & Book Shippers:

Kole Industries, Inc.
P.O. Box 520152
Miami, FL 33152
(800) 327-6085

Shipping envelopes also available
from "Jiffy Bag" dealers

Loose-leaf Binders:

Vulcan Binder & Cover Co.
P.O. Box 29
Vincent, AL 35178

All-Purpose Book Counter
Displays and Carriers:

S.L. Enterprises
443 E. Westfield Ave.
P.O. Box 292
Roselle Park, NJ 07204
(201) 245-8440

Beemak Plastics
7424 Santa Monica Bl.
Los Angeles, CA 90046
(213) 876-1770

Shelf Magazine Files, Desk
Organizers, Communication
Boards, Literature Trays:

Professional Aids
1678 S. Wolf Rd., Ste. 90D
Wheeling, IL 60090
(312) 459-6828

Binders, Report Covers,
Stationary & Memos,
Business Gifts:

Day-Timers
Allentown, PA 18001
(215) 395-5884

American Thermoplastic Co.
622 Second Ave.
Pittsburgh, PA 15219

NSC International
P.O. Box 1800
Hot Springs, AR 71902

Multi-Ad Services, Inc.
P.O. Box 786
Peoria, IL 61652

Stock Photos

Comstook
32 East 31st St.
New York, NY 10016

SPECIAL EQUIPMENT

*Automatic equipment that will affix
mailing labels to envelopes:*

Addressograph Farrington, Inc.
Randolph Industrial Park
Randolph, MA 02368-2698
(617) 963-8500

Headliner/Letter Writing Machines:

Kroy
P.O. Box C-4300
Scottsdale, AZ 85261

Printing/Typesetting Equipment:

Equipment Brokers Unlmtd.
3525 Old Conejo Rd., No. 105
Newbury Park, CA 91320

Telemarketing Machines:

Comtel Broadcasting Corp.
13 Harbourtown Center, Ste. 61
Noblesville, IN 46060

MARKETING SEMINARS

Russ von Hoelscher presents several intensive one- and two-day marketing seminars at leading cities in the United States and Canada throughout the year. Topics include: master mail order marketing techniques; self-publishing success strategies; "killer" advertising methods; and more. To get information on Mr. Hoelscher's upcoming seminars, write or call: Russ von Hoelscher Seminars, P.O. Box 546, El Cajon, CA 92022, (619) 282-5822.